SACRED TRUTHS

An Unveiled Path
to an Abundance of
Joy, Meaning & Love

TAMBRA HARCK

Sacred Truths

For information email:
office@TambraHarck.com

The author of this book does not dispense medical advice or prescribe the use of any technique as a form of treatment for physical, emotional, or medical problems without the advice of a physician, either directly or indirectly. The intent of the author is only to offer information of a general nature to help you in your quest for emotional and spiritual well-being. In the event you use any of the information in this book for yourself, which is your constitutional right, the author and the publisher assume no responsibility for your actions.

Photography by Marilynn Collin
Book cover design by James Balkovek, www.Balkovek.net

Printed, published and distributed in the United States by:
ONLE´International http://TambraHarck.com

Paperback ISBN: 978-0-615-38958-5

1st Edition, June 2010.
2nd Edition, August 2016

I paraphrase Hafiz when I say to you:

I tried the best I knew how
With my crude brushes, the tongue, these words,
To cover you with light.

To you.

Contents

PART IV : *Life Integration*

INTRODUCTION

Hello, my dear friend,

It was Saturday evening, a few weeks before my 50th birthday. I was sitting on the floor in my family room, cozied up in front of a fire, basking in a moment of glorious solitude. My day had been a quiet, private one: breakfast and a walk out on the pier with my beloved, Michael; a talk with my mother on the phone; simple chores around the house; a review of my notes for the next wave of writing this book. I felt joyous as I sat there appreciating the mysteries and mundane qualities of life.

From somewhere in space and time an awareness began to arise in me. I saw a person — a man, woman, or child, I can't be sure — a person who sat alone in their own home. Unlike me, this person had a heavy heart and a weariness about them. I sensed this person was not joyous, and in their solitude felt lost and separate.

This vision expanded — one more person in a room alone, then another. Then I sensed people who were out in public places, at dinner with their families, sitting in class, at church or at work. Some were in mid-conversation, others silent. Some were numb, others sobbing in their own private ways. I could feel them, see them, and hear them. Thousands and thousands of people around the globe, each one in sorrow, fear, worry or deep into feelings of despair.

For many years I was that person: lonely and lost. Mine was a busy, full, social and professional life; while privately I felt desperate and wanting to be hopeful. My striving to achieve and my spiritual searching were motivated by the emptiness I felt inside. I feel such compassion and love for the girl and woman I was then.

There I sat on my family room floor, tears filling my eyes with my hand at my heart. I knew in that moment that the people for whom I'm called to write this book will find it. They're asking for it, hoping, wanting to discover another way. Perhaps they haven't yet heard the voices of their own souls guiding them to lift themselves out of that deep, sorrowful, painful place.

If this is you, I hear you; I feel your pain. I want you to know there is another way: a joyous, loving, gracious and vital way to live. You don't have to take years to get there, like I once thought. There is no *"there"* to get to. It's in you right now. Whatever you want to experience: joy, love, abundance, peace, courage, health, grace, generosity, security, stillness, wealth, confidence, ease, creativity, communion with God... whatever you want to experience is yours.

You've likely heard that before. I had too — not just when I was in my lowest and numbest days, but also when I was coasting along, mildly impassionate about life. I argued, "If what I want is available to me here and now, I would have it. I would have love. I would have peace. I would feel joy and experience abundance. I would ..." blah blah blah. I looked for ways to mend this hurt, listening to tapes, setting goals, reading books, taking home-study courses and personality profile tests. But I was looking in the wrong direction — somewhere out there to tell me who I was in here. I learned a lot, but none of that changed how I felt, or the longing in my soul. In some ways it only left me even more disconnected and frustrated. Once I even argued with a voice on a recording when it said, "Abundance is all around you." Then I abruptly pressed the eject button.

That's how it is when we approach life with the narrow-mindedness of "I know that" or expect that what we want has to show up exactly in the way we say. We miss the mysteries. We refuse synchronicity, intuition and grace. We skip the critical step that requires us to act in alignment and conviction of our desires. Then we sit in rooms, weeping, wishing life were not so hard or lonely, not realizing that everything we desire is locked inside, and that the key to releasing it is in our own hands — our hearts and souls, our minds and bodies. We have forgotten our Selves. It is the human experience to forget the essential truths of all that is. A seeker's path is a call to remember.

> A call to...
> Re-member,
> Re-connect.
> Return to...
> The essence of who you are. You have access to the abundance of joy, meaning and love you desire.

Throughout this book I share with you profound, yet simple Sacred Truths. The word *truth* may conjure up ideas that I am a guru, or that I'm purporting to have all the answers. That is not the case. The one absolute Truth I hold is that you are a radiant soul, a person with unique gifts to express and share with the world.

Sacred Truths are defined and informed by cosmic and elemental laws that some may call Universal Principles or Divine Laws. I have spent my life as a student and teacher, seeking always to learn and apply, and offer discoveries as I unearth them. Mine is a soulful approach. I honor wholeness, seeing the richness of who we each are as inner-beings with outer-lives. An unveiled path traverses in both directions, inward and outward. Sacred Truths apply to our whole Selves.

With them I believe you can truly transform your life. That's a big statement, I know, "transform your life." It's not one I make lightly. I know — both from my own personal journey, and from the many thousands of clients and students I've worked with — that lasting and sustained transformation really can and does happen — even with the slightest shifts in your energy and awareness. Often, it is the slight shifts that bring about the deepest changes.

Whether you want to experience Prosperity, Joy, Love, Purpose, Belonging, Connection, Success, Beauty, Peace, Passion, Health, Creativity, Intimacy, a profound sense of WellBeing... in this book you will discover specific ways that you can do just that. As you discover for yourself Sacred Truths and integrate them into your life — any or all of these experiences can be yours!

Do you know who you are at the most fundamental level? ... The most inspired *(in spirit)* expression of you? That is a gift I want to share with you: **the radiance of your own soul ...** that you may **see it, know it, express it, embrace it. Live it. Live you.**

My intention is:

That I may serve you in the highest way possible, that if you choose, you may see your reflection here, and that you may open your heart and mind to the radiance of your soul, allowing the extraordinary Truth of your own magnificence to come fully, vitally awake in your life.

Soul-level exploration and transformative work interactive, a conversation of sorts. I invite you to read with an open mind and an open heart. Allow yourself to be informed. Take notes in the extra spaces in each section or draw pictures.

Read in the garden or at the water's edge. An unveiled path is a journey of the soul — not an intellectual concept. Engage with the ideas that get sparked in your awareness as you read.

This book is organized into four sections.

Part I is an introduction to *An Unveiled Path*, an invitation to unveil the radiance of your soul. You may notice that there are words throughout that are capitalized, like the word Love, and other words that are unusual, such as: WellBeing. In these cases, there is an emphasis on the word to enhance its meaning. It may not be grammatically correct, yet as I wrote, it was clear to me that it was important to take liberty with our language to bring the messages to print.

In Part II, you will find a chapter on each of the *Sacred Truths* that I am sharing with you. Volumes could be written on each of the six *Sacred Truths* that I present here. My intent is to share with you the essence the energetic quality and underlying wisdom that each of the Truths issues forth. They are written in poetic phrases, some are channeled expressions, some include stories or insights intended to guide you to discovering the meaning of Sacred Truths for yourself. This is the section you revisit when you want to remember, reconnect and return …

Part III, The Call to Continue, shows you ways to engage with Sacred Truths, to allow them to guide you along your journey. You will find some detailed processes that I have been using and teaching for years — and a new form of divine inspiration that has influenced my work, and this book, significantly.

In Part IV, you will find a variety of Life-Integration Practices that you can use — or be inspired by to create your own. The focus I have taken with the practices is to offer you options for integrating Sacred Truths in both inner and outer expressions, soulful and applicable. As you know, simply reading practices does not facilitate change. You must also act, whether through reflection-contemplation, embodied imagination, an exercise or a task. I welcome you to share your experiences with these or any Life-Integration Practices with me. (Find out how you can contact me in the Resources section.)

Part V is found in the large collection of videos I've created that are founded on the premise of the Sacred Truths covered here. You'll find many with practices, inspirations, or interviews on my website at TambraHarck.com/watch.

Volumes have been written — and passed down for thousands of years — carrying messages of Sacred Truths. You may have read many, and probably have some on your bookshelves right now, as I do. Still, with all that's been written, there is a challenge with using only written words. When we read we use only a fraction of our brains and virtually none of our *Being*.

Sacred Truths are founded on energetic principles. They are not a conceptual, intellectual endeavor. *Living* is full-bodied, interactive, engaging and experiential. I love leading live retreats for this very reason. What's possible when we are together — when we meditate, take walks, learn, dance, laugh, play together, explore, cry, witness one another — changes happen in more exponential and sustainable ways than they do when we read.

Sacred Truths

My prayer is that I present these Sacred Truths in such a way that you experience and integrate them — and live them in ways that bring you into an ever expanding abundance of joy, meaning and love.

Are you ready to unveil and shine your radiance into the world? I invite you to bring all your experience and wisdom to this moment, AND to be open. Allow yourself to FEEL, IMAGINE, DREAM, SENSE...

Be Well ~ In Joy,
Your Friend,

Tambra Harck

PART I:

An Unveiled Path

An Unveiled Path

We were made to enjoy music, to enjoy beautiful sunsets, to enjoy looking at the billows of the sea and to be thrilled with a rose that is bedecked with dew. Human beings are actually created for the transcendent, for the sublime, for the beautiful, for the truthful, and all of us are given the task of trying to make this... world a little more hospitable to these beautiful things.

— Arch Bishop Desmond Tutu

Do you remember seeing an old black and white movie — the scene when someone returns to a house that had been left unoccupied? All the furniture is still inside — left exactly as it had been while people were living there — except that everything is covered with cloths, large sheets and tarps are draped over all the beautiful furnishings. They covered all their valuables to protect them from the elements and the environment like dust and light.

When the caretakers return to the house, they begin to remove the cloths from furniture and art. As they pull away the protective cloths you see beautiful textiles, paintings, fine woodwork and sculptures. The room comes alive.

Imagine they returned to the house and forgot to remove the layers, leaving the cloths in place. All that richness and beauty would still be there, unseen, unappreciated, just below the surface. That's exactly what we do to ourselves. We cover our richly textured and colorful Souls. Our exquisiteness is hidden — often in plain view. Instead of old linens and tarps, our veils are made up of outdated, misplaced, inaccurate beliefs, compulsions, habits, illusions or lies that we perceive to be real.

You may feel uncomfortable thinking about *lies*. I assure you there is no need for judgment or blame. Actually, those responses only perpetuate lies. Many lies we live under were agreed upon and lived with for so long — and by so many that they seem to be true; they seem quite real. Often the veils you donned were simple agreements you made during the course of your life. Perhaps they fit the circumstances or surroundings at the time. Some lies you adopted from your family, community, society, dogma or a perception of history. You accepted them as the rules of belonging, and let yourself be directed by them. We all did. Then you added to the collection of lies with those you've told about yourself, about others, and about life.

Wisdom Key

An unveiled path continually reveals your infinite capacity for joy, love and prosperity.

Surprisingly, it requires conscious choice to see and know Truth, and not to lie. Without intention to discover and discard them, lies are pervasive and insistent. You — or your parents, culture or ancestors — may have needed them at some point, to protect your valuables — like the exquisiteness of your Soul — from the environment, so a protective veil was put in place. Unlike in the movie, no one returned to unveil your treasures. Over the years, more veils were added. You learned to see through the veils, not noticing that your vision was distorted, not realizing that whatever perceived danger may have lurked out there has likely passed.

So here you are, covered with veils — originally intended to protect you — that are now so familiar, you defend and protect them. Until ...

Until it is unbearable to remain shrouded. You choose to pull the veils away, revealing your true and glorious Self — for you and all to see. When you are ready to live fully, to celebrate your personal grace and share your unique gifts, lies just don't fit any longer. In that moment the black-and-white movie of your life is suddenly full color, high definition and 3D — and so are you!

An unveiled path continually reveals your infinite capacity for joy, for purpose, for love and abundance. As you allow habits, compulsions and personal beliefs that are based on lies to fall away, and as you internalize and practice Sacred Truths, you will discover that your life is your masterpiece, your expression of soul and radiance, creation and delight!

Wisdom Key

Your life is your masterpiece, your expression of soul and radiance, creation and delight!

Removing Your Veils

An unveiled path is simple, and illuminating. Unlike traditional therapeutic or analytical approaches, you don't need to focus on the "why" of each veil. You are a radiant and whole being — you are not broken or in need of dissection. You are whole and holy, perfect as you are. Sacred Truths guide you to reveal your radiance to yourself, and to the world around you.

Sacred Truths allow you to notice when something is obscuring your view, so that you can look beneath it and reveal your light and expression. If you need to inquire for clarification, it's only so you can withdraw your power from the veils.

What I'm sharing with you doesn't take a great deal of time, yet it is a lifelong journey. This is not a quick-fix approach to solving a problem in your life. You and your life do ***not*** need to be *fixed*. Every experience you have is a reflection of how you're seeing the world. Anything you define as a dilemma, challenge or set-back is simply a signal, calling your attention to veils — inviting you to remove them.

Sacred Truths continually reveal more of your potential and your radiance to you. Along this path you may awaken to experiences so exhilarating that you'll understand in your whole being exactly what Joseph Campbell meant when he said that what we really want is to, "feel the rapture of being alive." Rapture is not a word we often use. It means *a feeling of intense pleasure and joy*.

Imagine the experience of living your life in a state of rapture, of *feeling the intense joy and pleasure of being alive*. This potential awaits you. Actually, it is in you right now. Sacred Truths provide an illuminating map, guiding you to unveil yourself to this glorious, rapturous experience.

People say that what we're all seeking is a meaning for life. I don't think that's what we're really seeking. I think that what we're seeking is an experience of being alive, so that our life experiences on the purely physical plane will have resonances within our innermost being and reality, so that we actually feel the rapture of being alive!

— Joseph Campbell

Intuitive Discovery

You must learn one thing:
The world was made to be free in.
Give up all other worlds
Except the one to which you belong.
— David Whyte

Early on in my consciousness and spiritual studies, I thought I had to understand the details of my shadow, delve deeply into the stories and my life's wounds to be able to transcend from the habits, pain and beliefs that shackled me. I found many rich, inner discoveries as I did that level of excavation. Perhaps you've been on your own version of this treasure hunt. But even as I pursued my shadow, I was perpetuating a lie, two, in fact, that I merged together.

> Inaccurate Thought #1: Being personally accountable requires looking at my most hideous, ungracious, pitiful qualities and stories; and

> Inaccurate Thought #2: The only way to enlightenment or personal freedom was to look deeply into the muck and mire of my humanity.

My intuition told me there were alternatives to this approach, but I kept quiet about it. Instead I pursued my desire — to discover love, joy, a sense of WellBeing and authentic self-expression — by repeating to myself this question: "what's wrong with me."

Dark nights of the soul are often credited — after they have long since passed — as being a turning point, providing a glimpse into the shadowy recesses or resistances that were holding down the one who suffers. I have experienced many such nights, some lasting weeks, months or more than a year. While in those lowly, unlit crevices, there is no sense of "If I just wait this out, I'll pop out on the other side into joy and love." Literally, "dark night of the soul" means: all sense of consolation is removed. So while crises of faith can lead to new experience of perceiving light — or consciousness, they are not the only, or most freeing, ways to get there.

Wisdom Key

Sacred Truths are a direct path to joy, love and abundance.

Many spiritual seekers are obsessed with looking at and clearing their self-limiting thoughts, beliefs, behaviors, or blocks. In their swirl of perpetual self-analysis, they are not living. Life is on hold until the road is cleared.

My intuition showed me that there was a more direct route to the joy, love, intimacy, freedom and peace of mind I longed for. As I followed my intuition and divine inspiration, I discovered Sacred Truths. Along the path of this discovery, my old beliefs, veils that said I had to suffer to find my Self, dissolved. Today I have a consistent experience of joy. That does not mean that all the circumstances of my life are easy or satisfying. Rather, the joy that emanates from within me is not shrouded in as many veils.

Sacred Truths are a direct path to joy, love, abundance and so much more. As Sacred Truths emerge in your consciousness, lies that you have been living with can dissolve, swiftly and completely, no longer claiming your energy or your attention.

For many people, as they come to explore their spirituality or souls' calling, it's often in weary response to feeling "fed up" or out of sorts with the way they have been living. Perhaps they don't feel quite at home in their own skins, or that they belong in their family — with their friends or in their work. They may feel lost, lonely, frustrated or resentful. At some point, these feelings of discomfort reach a peak. Or they may catch a glimpse through the veil of consciousness, as in an "ah-ha moment," an epiphany or a revelation.

Whatever leads you to the next step along your journey, you are likely to find it becomes more uncomfortable to stay in what's familiar than it is to move into a new state of consciousness. As unfamiliar as this new state may be, life here is filled with new possibility and potential for the richness that emerges from soulful living.

Of course, you can choose to make it difficult and hard. Living in Truth is not hard. Resisting it is. I've had a lot of experience with resisting. My biggest leaps have been quick and clear; then as I began to grow into my expanded self, I struggled and made every turn difficult. Difficulty is often a sign that you haven't expanded your perception of yourself to live into this new perspective. Part of you still feels like you are your limited, former self. A gravitational pull draws you back to the old ways of being.

As you integrate Sacred Truths into your daily life, you expand and release the three-way push-pull of who you were — against who you are — against who you're becoming. Here I share with you ways of being that will remind you of your essential Self, and lead you to release the veils that have kept you from your Self, your Soul. And guide you to expand and grow.

A New Humanity

We call them "consciousness movements" because of their common intention to throw open the windows and doors of the musty old mind-sets we live in, shake the dust out of the covers we wrap around our bodies, and in a thousand old and new ways, guide whoever is willing to show up and pay attention to a fresh experience of being human.

— Paul H. Ray and Sherry Ruth Anderson

Many people from around the world are talking about a coming change in human consciousness and human potential. Some are calling it a "Global Shift" or a "Great Awakening." The conversation is lively, exciting and filled with uncertainty. There are ever-expanding perspectives; scientific discoveries and greater awareness coming to the surface, while systems and structures we've relied on are dissolving.

I have been aware since I was a young girl that we would see a significant change in the world in my lifetime, unlike anything humankind has ever experienced. I knew that I would play a part in the change — that many of us would.

People are awakening to expanded consciousness more readily and in greater numbers than ever before. The veil that has kept us collectively separate from Sacred Truths is thin — with big openings that thousands of people are now passing through with ease and grace.

It seems the collective veil is dissolving, and as it does, we are each being called to awaken to our individual magnificence, to live with purpose and generosity of spirit. If you are going to answer your call, I believe you must open your heart and mind and take mature responsibility for your choices.

We have an opportunity, unlike anything our ancestors had, to transcend challenges and divides that have plagued humankind for thousands of years. The choice is there each day, each moment — to welcome the opportunities before us, and to courageously live into our potential. Sacred Truths provide a path for doing just that, an *unveiled* path.

Wisdom Key

Open your heart and mind, and take mature responsibility for your choices.

Sacred Truths are timeless. You will be enriched by the wisdom you will gain from them, now and for the rest of your life — in ways you may not yet even imagine. If you notice that you feel strong in your understanding and embodiment of a Sacred Truth, use that strength to guide you to develop another.

One's spiritual journey is just that, a journey. There's no *"there"* to get to. There's no completion to a Sacred Truth — it's not like taking a test. The only time limit is how long you live. The experience of transformation is one of unfolding and un-layering while you blossom into your fullness. Each day brings opportunities for conscious intention, attention and action to living in alignment with Sacred Truths. Integrating Sacred Truths into your life, day by day, is a spiritual, soulful, symbolic dance.

Can you imagine: You and the Universe dancing a magnificent, joyous YOU into existence?

Wisdom Key

Integrating Sacred Truths into your life, day by day, is a spiritual, soulful, symbolic dance.

PART II

Sacred Truths

Sacred Truths

The First Sacred Truth :
You are Infinite and Powerful.

The Second Sacred Truth :
Your Body is the Temple of your Soul.

The Third Sacred Truth :
Soul Desire is Your Key to the Universe.

The Fourth Sacred Truth :
Love Is.

The Fifth Sacred Truth :
You are Not Your Veils.

The Sixth Sacred Truth :
Believe. Act in Faith. Trust.

THE FIRST SACRED TRUTH

You are Infinite and Powerful.

There is a light that shines beyond all things on earth, beyond us all, beyond the heavens, beyond the highest, the very highest heavens. This is the light that shines in our hearts.

— Chandogya Upanishad

You are the meeting place between the ethereal and material, the vast and the vascular. You are eternal, mystical and creator. You are timely, embodied expression. Both spiritual and physical. As such, you are an infinite and powerful being.

Mystics and enlightened beings have spoken of the oneness of all things, seen and unseen, tangible and intangible, for millennia. They have written songs and poems, chanted, danced, held Satsang to express this Sacred Truth, and to awaken others to its meaning. And they continue today.

Wisdom Key
You are as much the creation as the creator, infinite and powerful, embodied with unlimited possibility.

Along my own journey and discoveries, I've come to see that this one-ness, this inner and outer reflection of divine light, is found in everything and everyone, and that we are each made up of the same stuff, yet we are different. We are Divine and ordinary. All that exists does so as an expression of a mystery beyond what our bodies and minds can truly define or comprehend. You are as much the creation as the creator, infinite and powerful, embodied with unlimited possibility.

As you awaken to your divine consciousness, and the reflection of divinity in all that is around you, there is a grace and a power that you step into that forever changes the way you experience life. You can change, create, transform and grow, serve and honor the exquisite interconnectedness of all of life.

You may think, as many of us have, "Who am I to..." Or "What do I matter? I'm just one person." But you're not just one person. You are an infinite and powerful being! You are not separate and alone except as you resist your true nature.

Imagine you are looking through a lens. Gazing out, you see into an expanded space. That space is you, your life and beyond, and includes the entirety of the universe, the known and the mysterious of all that exists. Yes, you are that expansive: infinite and powerful. As you gaze out, can you feel, sense, and know that you create it all — the beauty, the conflicts, the inventions, the commerce: the everything?

Now, imagine the lens you are looking into is actually a microscopic mirror. Your gaze is directed inward where you see the miracle of your inner life. Your inner landscape is as expansive as the outer. It is known and mysterious, seen through your fantasies, your imagination, the functions of your body and the expressions of your soul.

Eternal light is both outer and inner, known and of the mysteries, and includes all the murkiness and shadows that are formed in response to that light. You are that infinite and that powerful.

A Call to Purpose

Your inner Light might be thought of as your Soul, your unique gifts or the spark of Spirit as it lives in you. Bringing your light to shine in and around you is your highest calling, a call to live your Soul's Divine Purpose.

Questioning that your life has meaning, that your passion, artistry, your soul has purpose beyond the ordinary-ness of your everyday experience is brought on by the veils you don.

This story expresses in a direct and powerful way what it means to honor and live your Purpose: Legendary choreographer, Agnes de Mille was a close friend of Martha Graham. Martha was both a dancer and choreographer, and is recognized as a pioneer of modern dance. One day Agnes confessed to her friend that she felt burning desire to be excellent, but had no faith that she could. Martha said to Agnes, and to each of us who awakens to our own calling,

> *There is a vitality, a life force, a quickening that is translated through you into action, and because there is only one of you in all time, this expression is unique. If you block it, it will never exist through any other medium and will be lost. The world will not have it. It is not your business to determine how good it is nor how valuable it is; nor how it compares with other expressions. It is your business to keep it yours clearly and directly, to keep the channel open.*

This is true whether you believe it is true or not. Your life matters. What you do with it matters. Strive to follow the ancient invitation: Know Thy Self. Continuously choose to keep the channel open. Dance, create and be guided by your unique expression. Be the exquisite gift that you are.

Wisdom Key

Your life matters. What you do with it matters.

Let yourself be guided in your BEING. Be open to your channel and act from it as you work, parent, design, start a business, play a sport, prepare a meal, volunteer, go to school, garden, make love, shop, travel, host a party. You see, Being Your Infinite and Powerful Self is not about what you do, it's about who you are. Allow your energy, your vitality to inform, infuse and inspire your actions.

Your gifts, your unique expression, your vitality are how you bring your infinite and powerful self to life! The age-old questions of spiritual seekers: "Who am I? What is the meaning of my life? Where did I come from? Why am I here?," all stem from this deep calling from within you, inviting you to tap into your infinite resources — Source — and bring it to the surface, to expression, to live your life with purpose.

Wisdom Key

Allow your energy, your vitality to inform, infuse and inspire your actions.

Your purpose doesn't define you or your value. Your purpose fuels you, informs you, reminds you that you are part of the mystery of life; that you matter and how you live matters. For years I struggled with this. I thought — like so many other spiritually oriented, productivity-minded people think — that I had to keep my spirit/soul yearnings to myself while I performed and produced with effort and skill. I didn't share my innate wisdom with the people in my life. Many of them saw it, they knew it, but I thought it was my "secret" and that it should be kept that way. I thought it would be out of integrity to use my gifts of intuition, or reading energy and pattern, in my business, or in my relationships, or in any way that wasn't specifically about my spiritual studies and experiences.

I was wrong, and clearly not aligned with being Infinite and Powerful. Your gifts are meant to aid you, lighten your burdens and light your way. I was stubborn, and to be fair, I was also informed by a personal lineage that believed it was not safe to be seen or heard in all that power. Perhaps it wasn't for them, then. Perhaps, as my mother says, I'm healing a deep wound that goes back in time through ancestral clan waves of seers, healers, seekers who experienced persecution, ridicule and worse.

You do not have to choose pain and struggle. I hope you hear better than I did, as I'm sure I was told this by both my inner and outer reSources countless times! You do not have to deny your connection to the infinite, to God, to Love. If you are struggling, I want you to hear this: Your struggle is a sign that you are resisting your Essence, or refusing your innate expression of Joy. Resisting your Essential Self creates the experience of suffering and struggle.

My Soul's Divine Purpose is, in part, to lift people who are suffering, in pain because they are living in a way that keeps them separate from the radiance of their own souls... to lift them out of that pain and suffering. To teach or guide them to do this for themselves — and in so doing, they transcend and experience their own radiance.

Looking back over my life, I can see that I have been doing and being my Purpose all along. I also continue to learn, gaining skill and experience so that I can BE even more of myself. That's how life works: You can choose to consciously participate, bringing a sense of meaning and purpose to your own expression.

Wisdom Key
Resisting your Essential Self creates the experience of suffering and struggle.

For over 35 years I was curious about Soul's Divine Purpose — mine, and also that of others. I felt a deep yearning to know my Purpose and to live it. I mistakenly thought I had to discover a password, learn a handshake, a wink or a nod — as if I were seeking to enter a secret chamber of a private club. The only secrets are held within, covered in veils. There is nothing you must learn or acquire from any outside source. Yet I believed there were trials I had to endure. At times I felt outright desperate in my seeking. What would I have to do before my Soul's Divine Purpose would be revealed to me?

When I finally relaxed and heard the eternal voice of wisdom from within, I discovered that my Purpose wasn't some deep secret, hidden from me. It was in me, in plain view, simply waiting for me to come home to myself, to become trustworthy with myself and with my gifts. This, I know, is the simple truth for each of us. It is the wisdom expressed in this, The First Sacred Truth: You are Infinite and Powerful.

You might think of your Soul's Divine Purpose as a lifelong friend. It has been with you since you began and will never abandon you. Your Soul's Divine Purpose has faith in you.

I have spoken with thousands of people about their Soul's Divine Purpose, or their longing to know it, live it, consciously and by choice. The fundamental longing to know that your life has meaning — that you matter and how you live matters — is a compelling force, propelling you from within to shed any veils that prevent you from seeing, being, living your full radiance.

Wisdom Key

You can choose to consciously participate, bringing a sense of meaning and purpose to your own expression.

Your Soul's Divine Purpose is unique to you. It may or may not determine your profession, or the role you play in your community, family, or the world. It may be similar to the purpose of someone else or even of thousands of others, but your very specific Soul's Divine Purpose is yours and yours alone. Only you can say yes or no to living it. Only you have the power of that choice. And if you say yes, and continue to be informed and engaged with your purpose, it will continue to expand — or heighten or deepen — inviting you into new realms of expression. You will be continuously invited to learn, create, release and persevere, as you grow, and to follow your own Soul's longing and intention.

I've wondered what I could tell you about "finding your Purpose." While it is work I often do with my clients, guiding them to explore in soulful ways the expression of their Souls' Divine Purpose, it is not my calling to write about it — at least not at this time. In Section IV: Life-Integration, you'll find a collection of practices and resources to aid you in integrating this and each Sacred Truth into your life.

The Choice is Yours

There is a longing that lives in each of us. It is imprinted into our being, as unique as our fingerprints or DNA. It's a one-of-a-kind spark that lives in you, the radiant, exquisitely beautiful gift you were born to bring into the world. Science and in-depth studies have been uncovering evidence that shows how our bodies carry this miraculous information. I see it as the wisdom of the ages living in our consciousness, in our bodies and beings, waiting for as long as it must until we choose to honor and access it.

For instance, fingerprints develop when a fetus is between the 14th and 16th week of development, and they never change. While your fingerprints can be damaged or destroyed, they don't change. I find that intriguing. Apparently, so too did Richard Unger, founder of the International Institute of Hand Analysis. Following his fascination for palmistry, his studies led him to discover dermatoglyphics, the study of fingerprints. After 25 years of research, he asserts in his book, *LifePrints,* "...fingerprints are a soul-level imprint," and provide "a life-purpose map that can be used as a daily compass." You may well have chosen your Purpose, a way in which your life would have meaning, long before you were born.

It's different with DNA. You probably grew up learning in school, like I did, that your DNA is unique to you, rare and filled with information. I was taught that it determines how we look, grow, age, learn, develop, heal, and so on — and that it stays the same throughout your life. Scientists have been discovering new understandings about the inner workings of our bodies, in DNA, as well as in the brain. They seemed to be surprised by how differently the inner-scape of our bodies function, compared to what they thought even just a decade ago. Significant discoveries now indicate that our DNA does change. It isn't predetermined and unchanging. Our genes change as influenced by environment and perception. We transform on a soul-level in much the same way:

> By altering your perceptions of your environment,
> you change your experience, your life ... yourSelf.

Neurologists and neurophysiologists have been studying the brain, and its responses to a range of stimuli, including thoughts, images and words for many years. This will not likely surprise one who practices meditation, or one who prays with an uplifted perception of God, or one who focuses their attention consistently on a joyous, loving, meaningful life. The findings of this research show that thinking about, pondering, contemplating big ideas like God, Peace, Love, or something that you value most highly, physically changes the make up of your brain.

This sounds a lot like what scientists have determined to be true with DNA ... that when you alter your perceptions, you change your experience. If you ponder a value that holds meaning for you, what Mark Robert Waldman, author and researcher, calls "the big idea." In his neuroscientific research, Mark reports that when you simply focus on a "big Idea," a thought like compassion, peace, joy, love, well-being, a sacred belief, you will change the structure and function of your brain. Actually, change your brain!

I'm not a scientist, so I realize I'm taking some liberties with this information. What's really fascinating, synchronistic and fabulous about all this — at least to me, is: mystics, artists, alchemists, naturalists and many other observers and participants in life have known for ages that when you alter your perception of your environment, you alter your behavior, your beliefs and your experiences. You are always, ALWAYS, capable of transforming your experiences because you are both ethereal and material.

How you express your Purpose is entirely up to you. The choice is yours. There is vitality in you, a spark or light, an expression that only you can bring to life. The question is: Will you?

Wisdom Key

You are unique and individual, continuously creating your own experience.

You are an Infinite and Powerful Being. You are made up of the same miraculous, wondrous stuff that forms everything and everyone. You are not separate from the most profound expressions of beauty, joy, love and awe. You are unique and individual, continuously creating your own experience. Connected, whole, integrated, and exquisite!

THE SECOND SACRED TRUTH

Your Body is the Temple of Your Soul.

So great is the bliss and repose of the soul, that even the body most distinctly shares in its joy and delight.

Theresa von Avila

Metaphysically speaking, if you were a devotee, caring for the temple where your community came to pray and hold ceremonies, you would love the space, clean it, adorn it and bless it. You might use music, incense or the sounding of bells to move the energy. There would be candles lit as the symbolic expression of enlightenment. You would tend to the temple's needs with conscious intention and attention. Your body deserves nothing less – for it is a temple, your sacred space, where you come to pray, to celebrate and ceremoniously live the days of your life — even the most ordinary, mundane of your days.

Most of us have forgotten to honor our bodies and our environments in this way — or perhaps we never knew it was possible. We choose numbing, deadening, neglectful or even abusive behaviors and fill our time and space with doing, getting, having, keeping, thinking or recovering. Plus, we are subjected to our conveniences — the electronics, processed foods and chemicals we use in everyday life — and the resulting pollution, garbage and energy drains on our physical and energetic WellBeing. When you change your relationship with and the treatment of your body, you change both your own personal, immediate environment and the global, expanding environment, creating a ripple effect from your actions and intention.

Your magnificent body is a gift, complex and mysterious, and yet so familiar to you. Your body is the nexus of your experience of life — the vehicle that allows you to *experience being* alive.

As The Temple of Your Soul, your body is the gateway to Being. Passage through that gateway requires very simple, aligned actions: primarily to care for and attend to your body, your energy and your surroundings.

It is honoring to your *temple* when you appreciate your body. Enjoy visceral experiences of being alive that can only be lived, not thought or imagined. Through softened senses and heightened awareness, your body provides you access to innate wisdom, intuition and the capacity to heal. You can transform energy into experience.

Wisdom Key

Your body is the gateway to Being.

You must have a room or a certain hour of the day or so where you do not know what is in the morning paper. A place where you can simply experience and bring forth what you are or might be... At first you might think nothing is happening. But, if you have a sacred space and take advantage of it and use it everyday, something will happen.

— Joseph Campbell

Body's Wisdom

Many years ago, as I was preparing to enter a personal-spiritual ritual, I became aware of a great resistance welling up in my body. I was committed to entering this transformation as consciously as possible, which meant I wasn't going to ignore my body's message. It seemed to be screaming, "No, I don't want to!"

Outside in the desert night, alone, the moon as my witness, I began a dialog with my body. This was a form of what's called *active imagination,* a meditation technique developed by Carl Jung. I often use this practice to understand and discover inner motivations or resistance, or even to access divine wisdom. Instinctively, I knew that my body and I could have a conversation that would help me build a bridge between my resistance and my intention.

I asked my body why it was resisting. My body said it was afraid that if I expanded into higher consciousness, I would abandon it, that I would degrade physical ecstasy and creative expression. As this dialog continued, I heard its concerns. I honored it and agreed. It had evidence to warrant those fears. I assured my body that no matter what came about, unless I died in the ritual or as a result, I would still need it. I would honor it. Then I asked it to forgive me for the ways I had abandoned and abused it, and to support me as I stepped into and through this ritual-initiation.

Wisdom Key

Honor your body as your sacred space, your temple.

As we completed, my body's wisdom gave me a manifesto for honoring the temple of my soul. I share it with you here, as a gift from my body-soul to you. This is nearly unchanged from the original message.

Breathe — full deep inhales, complete exhales. Breathe with awareness that infusing this body with breath rejuvenates and inspires. Be where air is fresh and clean. Feel the rhythm of breath contract and expand. Appreciate the miracle of breath.

Hydrate — drink pure, clean water. Throughout the day, every day, drink with awareness that this body's eternal fountain is being replenished. Bathe, soak and refresh in water. Visit and gaze upon great bodies of water often.

Nourish — eat for nourishment. Listen with special attention to this body's need for nourishment. Choose fresh, whole foods that come from the ground, that have been kissed by sun and dew and that vibrate with life-giving energy. Eat with awareness that this body is being infused with pleasure, fuel and information. Be present for ecstatic experiences through scent, taste and texture of food. Plant and grow organic herbs and vegetables. Nurture that which nourishes.

Touch and Be Touched — intentional, loving, invigorating touch. Touch with awareness that this body is the beloved. Even in the most basic gestures of cleansing and grooming, touch and feel the touch as love. Touch and receive the loving touch of others. Receive healing, energizing, soothing and invigorating touch. Hold a hand. Caress a face. Hug. Kiss. Human contact. Animal contact. Earth, air and water contact.

Note: It's interesting that the body-wisdom offered me at the time did not mention anything about sex. I didn't yet know I would soon begin a personal four year ritual of celibacy. One might think that celibacy is void of erotic and sensuous expressions, and that may the be case for some, but it wasn't for me. I discovered soul-level sexual and intimate and orgasmic expressions of being that I had never been open to when there was the distraction and outlet of a lover. One such expression happened as I was walking through the organic garden of a private retreat center in Napa Valley. I sensed the life force in a freshly picked wild strawberry. Bringing it to my mouth, I felt the texture, warmth and wetness of the fruit. A feeling of ecstasy washed through, over and around me as it released its flavor onto my tongue. As my monastic life came to an end, sexual, sensuous contact and expression was added to Touch and Be Touched — with new meaning and presence than had been true for me before.

Move — move for breath, release, expression and energy. Move with awareness and intention that this body is a magnificent multi-dimensional map of bones, blood, muscles, organs, and other such forms of interworking matter. Move with awareness, too, that there is light and space between the cells of this body. Moving allows light and energy to flow in and through this body. Move to breathe hard. Move to gain strength. Move to sweat. Move to release and eliminate. Move to express emotion, channel energy and live in Purpose. Move in appreciation for this body's expression, beauty, power and subtlety. Dance the elements. Hike. Bike in nature.

Presence — be present to what is. Be still. Have quiet in each day. Unplug from your perpetual state of doing, going, planning, calculating, labeling and defining. Experience the being-ness of others, animals, trees, the moon, a canyon, a stream and the sky.

Nature — be in the outdoors. Nature is the great teacher, reflecting natural rhythms and cycles of life. Observe, engage and experience nature. Be witnessed by the moon. Allow the sun's warmth to shine on hair and skin. Feel the mist of fog and drops of rain. Walk barefoot. Swim in the oceans. Plant flowers, trees, vegetables and herbs.

Sleep — rest and restore. Get ample, quiet, peaceful, restorative sleep. Sleep clear of electronics and stimulants. Make time for dreaming and exploring dreams. Go to bed with a clear mind, appreciative — and early. Rise with the sun.

Sound — be mindful of sound and vibrations. Sounds all around and those of the voice carry vibrations and move energy. Sing and speak with gratitude and grace. Listen to and play music to soothe, heal, inspire, de-crystallize and inform. Bask in the sounds of silence.

Play — lighten up! Playfulness does a body good. Laugh. Play joyfully and with a light heart. Play in this body — toss a ball, dig in dirt, silly dance, draw pictures without looking. Create for the fun of creative expression.

Environment — have sacred space for everyday living. See the environment in which this body lives as sacred. Create spaces that protect this body from the elements; excite and engage the senses; have light, space and perspective. Expand this practice to clothing, housewares, furnishings, people and even entertainment. Be aware of the energy of this body's surroundings. Create beauty all around.

Note: We did not yet have the extensive technology we have today when I received the Body-Wisdom. I have received more guidance since then, suggesting that I use electronics as consciously as possible, not to wear a mobile phone on my body, or hold portable phones to my head; to move away from the computer and other forms of technology that emit electromagnetic fields frequently.

Since that moonlit night in the high desert, I have embodied and later forgotten some of the wisdom offered to me — only to remember again. Much of what was revealed to me is universal, wisdom that serves all bodies. You may choose to incorporate these practices into your life. They are transformational, particularly to those of us in the industrialized world. These are not a "to do" list for health and fitness. They are about intention and presence, not specifically about the *doing*. Our bodies are energetic, ever changing, healing and growing, responsive to our thoughts, emotions, surroundings, intentions and our actions. These practices are a roadmap to *being*.

Wisdom Key

Listen to your Soul through softened senses, open and curious.

Energy Systems

I had been going to churches for many years, but never specifically for the teachings or tenets. When I was 10 years old I joined an Episcopal church around the corner from our house because I heard a choir from outside and I wanted to sing. Before that I went to bible study with my best friend's family at a Baptist church. At an even earlier age, my family lived in San Francisco, where my aunt, Emma Lou, took me, my sisters and our cousins to a variety of churches and temples on Saturdays and Sundays. Then we'd spend an afternoon in Golden Gate Park or at Ocean Beach. The experience of church, voices in harmony, family outings and museums all blended together for me.

The first time I heard and felt the resonance of the phrase, "Your body is the temple of your soul," I knew, clearly, that this was Truth. It rang through me. I remember being surprised that someone else knew it too. I was 11, and was having a conversation with two men from a local Church of Jesus Christ of Latter Day Saints church, more commonly known as Mormons.

That was perhaps the beginning of my conscious Body-Wisdom journey. The many professions and passions I have pursued since then have a common thread running through them, each exploring energy systems that express through the body. I have been honored to lead thousands of people to discover the wisdom of their own bodies, and living and teaching Body-Wisdom as an expression of my Soul's Divine Purpose.

Through our bodies we "know" the earth. We know its rivers, its valleys and its pulsing oceans. We know its raging fires, loss and death. We know the emergence of new life in our bodies just as the earth knows new land, the birth of a foal, a budding tree. We know its spaciousness and its density. Our bodies know the quaking and eruptions that begin from somewhere far below the surface. Earth is an energy system — as are all the elements, such as Fire, Water, Air and Ether. The seasons are an energy system that we witness and participate in internally and externally, repeatedly — and cyclically.

Wisdom Key

Energy systems express through the body.

Other energy systems that engage Body-Wisdom include the Chakra system, Voice Dialog, Yoga, the Enneagram, Hand Analysis, body meridians, archetypes, and many Universal Principles. Functional body systems such as digestion and the lymph also serve us with heightened and deepened wisdom when we simply discover how to listen and engage with them.

The Language of Your Soul

Your body is an ideal link to your soul. If you want to listen to your soul, soften your senses; allow an openness and curiosity to guide you to discovering a new language. This language speaks through dreams and intuition, through symbol, image, sound, storytelling, music, dance, and play. Your soul understands the rhythms of nature, honors wholeness and union, expanding in ever wider, deeper, higher expressions of love, joy and wisdom. This is the only "foreign" language I am fluent in — and I trust that there is so much more to discover about the language itself and what it has to offer.

Coming Home to Your Self — A Woman's Journey

While a man can — and many do — discover his spiritual path through the body, it is the primary gate for a woman. Through dance, gardening, cooking, play, song, and other forms of creative expression, we, as women, return to our essence. I have known many women who at mid-life began to paint or sculpt or write sensuous poetry, and found in these expressions a lifeline that led them home to themselves.

Do you hear the call to come home to your Self, your body, your soul?

I find that most women who have lived in a masculine-ruled, patriarchal environment, and adopted the postures and drive of that energy, see their bodies as instruments, machines or masses of flesh and bones, to be conquered, measured and ruled. A time comes when she begins to recognize that her body is also subtle, energetic, creative and powerful in a different way than she knew before. It may even come by surprise: during a yoga class she might realize somewhat suddenly that the asanas she's been doing every week are not so much about strength, flexibility, balance and endurance, but rather about the energy that's moving through her, and her ability to allow the energy to flow. In that moment she begins to come home to her body, to her soul.

No matter how familiar she is with the workings of her body, it now seems different, and perhaps uncomfortable, scary, nauseating. She has a new awareness of her intuition, her authentic voice, but she's not sure what to do with them yet. If you've been living 25, 35 or 55 years unaware of the experience and energies, joys and wisdom you can access through your body, it's easy to react by resisting or even rejecting this new experience. It was for me. The first time I was invited into a woman's dance, there were perhaps 100 or more women joining in a dance of the feminine. I would not move from my seat. I sat there, a frozen stone, refusing to join in their dance. I was clutching the sides of my chair to assure I wouldn't get up. Yet I felt the stir in me, the yearning to be my Self, fully, and while I'd never experienced it in that way before, I quietly, from somewhere deep inside (covered with many layers of veils), felt the call to dance.

Wisdom Key

Do you hear the call to come home to your Self?

To dance in this way is not about being seductive,or in time with the music. There are no steps to follow. This form of dance, as with any soul's expressions, comes from a source or connection from within, perhaps, too, with something ancient.

In the years that followed, I found courage, permission, and later expression through my dance, literally dancing my body, sometimes with music, sometimes in silence, alone and with other women, with men and women, even with the wind! Inviting others to discover their bodies in this soulful way, I dance.

You may paint or garden. Perhaps you will write or sculpt or swim in the ocean, or hike and open to your presence as you sense the presence of your natural surroundings. You may read poetry aloud, allowing the images of the words to touch you and resonate through you.

Maybe you will, as my friend Joan has, discover a new way of "being yourself" when you play with your grandchild. Or perhaps you'll be drawn to create heart-felt connections with others as you go on about your otherwise ordinary days.

None of this is about losing yourself in the pleasantries of life, although you may want to do just that. This soul-level connection to your body will bring you more fully into the experience of who you truly are. If you have been denying Her, the feminine principle, and identified, unconsciously, only with the drive and pragmatic focus of your masculine perspective, all this may sound frivolous. It is not *his* path: it is not your inner masculine's role to facilitate your body-soul connection. (Although, if you're anything like me, "he" will, over time, be quite appreciative of you, and who "she" is in you.) These aspects of the feminine and masculine are not about your physical gender, man and woman. Both are present in each of us, regardless of gender or sexual orientation or preference.

"The great work of our time is to bring the feminine into this culture," Marion Woodman, Jungian analyst and author, is quoted as saying in an interview for O Magazine. Marion is a long-time, long-distance teacher of mine for whom I have great appreciation, even though we've never met. She said the feminine is brought in "...in the most personal ways. Take time to listen to your dreams, to write them down. Take time to recognize that there are things going on within you that need to be felt, or said, or lived, or grieved. Pay attention to these things both in yourself and in the people in your life. Pay attention to the authentic self." As you integrate this Sacred Truth: Your Body is the Temple of Your Soul, take time with your Self.

Tapping the Well

You and I come from the bodies of our parents, quite literally, who come from the bodies of their parents, and so on and so on, back to the beginning of humankind. Before that, came the earth and all her creatures. This lineage gives some people access to body-soul connections through their sensitivity to the rituals, stories and cultures of their ancestors. Others communicate with and bring forth the wisdom of the animals, birds, reptiles, or the elements, such as trees, wind, fire, metal or blossoms. Meditating, journaling, dancing or practicing active imagination are all approaches that can bring you to this body-soul wisdom.

There is an ancient and deep well of wisdom from which you can find nourishment, nurturance, love, healing, forgiveness, understanding and peace. It is all available to you through the grace and miracle of your body.

Physical and Energetic Environment

Does your physical environment, where you live, work, play — how you dress, who you spend time with — does it all reflect the radiance of your soul? Did it ever occur to you that it could, or that when it does that it will nurture you on a deep, personal level by reflecting back to you that which is most exquisite about you?

I think of those images you've seen of a mirror that's reflected in a mirror, echoing images that take you in and in and in, and then bring you out. Your environment reflects you back to yourself, which in turn reflects you, amplified, back out into your environment. Being intentional and soulful about the environment you create further expresses that your Body is the Temple of Your Soul. Your body, and your surroundings — physical and energetic, conversational and relational, mystical and mundane — are the temples of your Soul.

Wisdom Key

Create environments that reflect the radiance of your Soul.

When I was around 20 years old I started on a journey that I didn't have a conscious understanding of until decades later. Intuitively, I discovered the value and benefits of creating environments that reflect the radiance of one's soul. No one was talking about this back then, and neither was I, yet somehow it was what I began doing when I started a catering company. As I met with each new client, the approach I had to creating their events was not about the menu, the timeline or the color scheme.

I wanted to know first: What was the underlying reason for the event? I would ask questions that guided my clients to express their souls' intentions for the gatherings with their family or their community. What experience did they want to create as they came together in celebration, appreciation or collaboration? At the event we would do more than just feed their guests or entertain them. We created an environment that physically and energetically affected the clients and their guests, through their senses and awareness, through the energy in the space. The process of discovery and creation was the same whether the event was for 2 or 2500.

You see, The Temple of Your Soul really has been an intrinsic lesson for me, and an expression of my Soul's Divine Purpose.

A wealth of wisdom lives within the mystery of your body, your temple. Every experience you've ever had, physically, emotionally, environmentally — even through thought — is energetically remembered in your body. Those experiences can be relived and redefined, even healed. Be gentle and courageous. Explore with curiosity and compassion. Above all, find and express your loving appreciation for your body — in whatever way you feel it. Your body wants to be loved by you, tended to as the Temple of Your Soul

THE THIRD SACRED TRUTH

Soul Desire is Your Unique Key to the Universe.

None of us will ever accomplish anything commanding except when he listens to this whisper which is heard by him alone.

—Ralph Waldo Emerson

Imagine a beam of light that emanates from within, your essence as an Infinite and Powerful being. Soul Desire comes up from the well of your being.

Soul Desire leads you to create experiences and opportunities that allow you to express and fulfill your Soul's Divine Purpose. When you experience Soul Desire, it is your light shining in and around you. It flickers and sparks, igniting energy charges that you feel as desire.

Wisdom Key
Soul Desire comes up from the well of your being.

Resonance of Desire

On my meditation altar I have a Tibetan singing bowl. When I slowly rub the wooden wand around the outer rim, the bowl begins to sing, emanating a resonance, a vibrational tone that is unique to the bowl. This is the sound it was designed to make. The materials it's made of, its shape and carvings, how I rest the base on my hand, the size of the wooden wand and how I hold it, even the room I'm sitting in — each of these elements, and more, come together to create this particular sound, this vibrational tone.

Soul Desire is the sounding of a bell. You have a vibrational tone: the resonance of your soul. As the bowl sings its unique sound, the resonance of your soul expresses your essence, your unique music — the vibrational tone of your Soul Desire. As you learn to sense your own resonance and become sensitive to noticing when it's vibrated externally, you move closer to your Soul Desire while it moves closer to you.

Whoever you are, or whatever it is that you do, when you really want something, it's because that desire originated in the soul of the universe. And, when you want something, all the universe conspires in helping you achieve it.

— Paulo Coelho

One woman I worked with privately, Darlyn, came to me at first because she wanted to be true to her soul. She said, "I miss who I am. Do I even know who that is? I long for peace in my heart." She was feeling lost to herself, resentful and like a failure. Life around her seemed to be disintegrating. I asked of her desire. She said, "I don't want to be held back. I am afraid of success. I don't want people to pull away from me."

The question was, "What do you want? What do you desire?" That's not the question she answered, as you can see.

Donna wasn't alone in this somewhat sad response. Habit and environment, and her personal veils of resistance, were in place, hiding her desire from her. She didn't even realize she was answering a question I didn't ask.

Wisdom Key

Sense your own resonance, and become sensitive to when it's vibrated externally.

She sensed her desire to have a different experience of herself and her life; she simply couldn't yet navigate her way toward identifying it. I designed a few Life-Integration Practices to help Donna develop awareness and skill, grounded in this Sacred Truth. One of her practices was to listen to the Grounding-Heart Meditation that I recorded for her a few times a week. Then as she awoke each morning, her life-integration practice was to feel herself, present, embodied, connected to the earth, and to ask herself, "What do I want? What do I truly desire?" Asking questions such as these with an open heart and softened senses, Donna soon found a more resonant place within from which she could hear, feel, intuit. From there answers emerged. Answers that were not just thoughts and ideas that she was expected to want, or what she believed she was worthy of wanting.

A few weeks later, I asked, "What do you want?" This time there was a brightness in her voice as Donna shared visions of a new home, of healing family upsets with her siblings. She wanted to enjoy being with her son who in a few months would leave for college. She wanted to open to possibility. She wanted to bring beauty and healing to the world.

It's not that Donna became optimistic. She turned her attention to her desire for growth, for connection and for enjoying life. Life-Integration Practices are often so subtle that you might think, "This doesn't work." Like Donna discovered, you too have an inner resonance with your Soul Desire. Ask yourself with curiosity, and then listen with softened senses.

As for Donna, she has a new, reliable connection to her intuition, and follows it. This alone changed Donna's outlook and the experience of creating her life anew. A year after that early conversation, Donna called to let me know she moved to San Diego to be near her brothers and their families. She started her new design business. The healthiest she's been in over a decade, this woman is in love with her creative and colorful life.

That's what is possible when you attune to Soul Desire.

What Do You Desire?

When you quietly, courageously allow yourself to feel what you want — not what others want of you or what you think you're supposed to want — what do you really want?

Feel your desire as it wells up in you. Notice as it is reflected through your senses, in your dreams, as you fantasize. There are no rules about what you can want or what's a worthy desire. Soul Desire emerges from your Soul. If it's a loving, committed relationship you want, or a piece of jewelry, to travel the world, to have a baby, to live alone, to start a business, or to give away all your possessions and go on a trek; to cut your hair, or hire a housekeeper, to swim in the ocean, drive a race car, etc. your desire is yours alone: Yours and the Universe's.

Listen to your inner voice, your intuition, a tingling perhaps, that draws your attention toward Desire. Shine your light in that direction. Be gentle and persistent, curious and courageous.

Wisdom Key

There is no one way to light your path.

Becoming present to True Desire can feel vulnerable, tender, scary, exhilarating. Soul Desire leads you into the unfamiliar and the unknown. Feelings of discomfort are to be expected, though those feelings do not need to stop your desire nor your motion. It's simply that you will be asked to grow, to release, to change and adapt so that you can create a new Reality. Trust that you are being shown a way to grow, expand and improve. Breathe and play with this!

It may sound simple — or even selfish — to focus on what you want. It is profoundly simple. And it is *selfish* in the best sense of the word: *Self,* capital S, Self - ish. True Desire honors and brings your Soul's Divine Purpose into expression.

Imperfect Pictures

Here's where a lot of people trip up. They expect to know exactly what they want. They want every last detail about when and with whom, and how they're going to get it. Goal setting classes have taught this too, right? Soul Desire is not a goal. Soul Desire can be an idea or a feeling or a place or an experience, an energetic vibration. It may involve a destination or an acquisition. It may lead to a goal. You might find that your Soul Desire starts with a feeling or an imagination, a tingling or some other sense of a calling, a longing or yearning.

You can only ever start where you are. If you cannot yet spread out your whole dream/desire as a full-color motion picture on the vision-board of your mind with timelines and action plans, that's okay. Many people follow their Soul Desires, never seeing or planning specifically in advance.

Wisdom Key
Soul Desire honors and brings your Soul's Divine Purpose into expression.

My friend Diane said, the first time we met, "I follow the energy." She experiences Soul Desire as a path, clearing the way, guiding her along through experiences and opportunities. When she describes her Soul Desire in business, she talks about using her innate gifts, how she relates to other people, the qualities of the people who show up as support, clients, resources and staff. She talks about relationships. For Diane, it's all about the feeling quality and the experiences she has with other people. As she is a business consultant, you might imagine she'd be more pragmatic and systematic in defining her business and growth — and she is when it comes to action. Soul Desire is not about actions or to-do lists. It's not about "how."

The intent here is to identify and follow the vibrational quality of what you want. Diane does it by feeling. Feelings, emotions are another way to experience vibration. I invite you to focus on your Soul Desire, follow the vibration of it, and let your imagination join in — like it's a game. The vibrational tone or resonance and the feelings and imaginations you have about what it would be like to have your Soul Desire be your Now Reality... That's where the magic lies! That's how it seems to Diane, like magic.

Soul Desire is the place where your Soul and the Soul of the Universe are saying to each other, "Yes, let's!" It can also feel tender, frightening, nerve-wracking or shameful. All types of emotions can arise when you set your sights on new experiences. Sacred Truths give you inner and outer skills and energetic awareness to respond to your emotions. For now, I encourage you to incorporate the experience of being on the other side of these feelings as you imagine the reality.

I lead groups of women and men in retreat settings to find and follow their Soul Desire. A few years back, Cindy returned to one of these retreats. During one session she kept getting this message: healer.

"It really took me by surprise," Cindy recalls, "But it also felt really right. I remembered a dream a long, long time ago."

"In the dream I was in Calcutta, holding a wasted body of somebody who was still alive. I was having mixed feelings about it." She laughs nervously as she recounts the dream, "Mother Teresa's voice came to me loud and clear, 'They are human. We must love them.'

"The dream was like a clarion call to me. I didn't know what to do with it at the time, but I could always hear that voice reverberating. That's the connection I made when I later heard the message: healer."

Wisdom Key

Imagine in your mind and body:
What will it be like to LIVE your
Soul Desire…

She carried this dream with her for many years. At the retreat she felt ready to claim it as her Soul Desire. She felt courageous and supported by her Infinite-Being-Self, and by the environment of the retreat.

Imagination is powerful beyond measure. With it we can harness, direct and follow energy. During the retreat Cindy imagined herself a healer, offering healing touch to others. She imagined in her mind and her body what it would be like to live this Soul Desire. When she was ready, she ritualized her intention to "make it so." A year later she returned to a workshop with me, and shared "It is so." Her study and practice of Healing Touch continues today.

Cindy's experience unfolded to her over time, while we see with Diane that Soul Desire can be uncovered from moment to moment. There is no one way, no right way to light your path.

Short Circuiting Desires

Michael and I were invited to a festive summer party with live music, children swimming and a lavish catered buffet. Our hosts had been busy for years, between traveling and remodeling their home. Now that the house was finished and they were in town, they decided to invite people from all their communities to a celebration. It was a wondrous gathering of families, couples and singles.

Meeting and talking to people about their lives and loves is a great joy for me. I met a woman, Suzanne*, at this party. She was really interested in what I do, and she shared with

* Some names have been changed to honor privacy.

me some of her joys and accomplishments in life. She and her husband passed along the business they built and ran for nearly 30 years to a son who was doing well. They recently bought a new home. She was healthy and fit — and was happy to be exploring this new phase of her life: retirement. It was fun to talk to someone who was intrigued by learning and growing... and not drifting off into the sunset.

I noticed a most interesting thing as we spoke. First, Suzanne got very excited, telling me how much she loves painting, how she wants to paint, and to learn and grow in her creative expression. She told me about her friend who painted beautifully, how inspired she was by her friend. She even bought a copy of *The Artist's Way*, and tried some of the exercises for freeing her creativity.

We each have an innate desire to create. It's in our human nature. Whether you create a beautiful home, start a family, plant a garden, start a business, fund a service organization, even design your wardrobe, or write a book... We have a fundamental need to create — and to grow. I loved hearing her passion as this woman told me about the freedom and creativity she felt when painting.

Wisdom Key

We have a fundamental need to create and to grow.

Then she seemed to get very worried by something I said. Right before my eyes I watched Suzanne change from exuding an energy of passion and creativity to showing worry and judgment. It was as if the wiring that fed her passion suddenly crossed over to judgment. She became VERY concerned as she thought about people following their passions, developing their unique gifts and being empowered by their divine-lights. She seemed to think that if people (Who? Herself, me, her grown children? Our world leaders?) developed an appreciation for and commitment to living in accord with their soul's calling, or their unique magnificence, that somehow they would become "pillow-y."

That's the word she used: Pillow-y.

Her judgment crept in. I remember hearing — and thinking — thoughts like this before; that idea that if we "follow our bliss," as Joseph Campbell used to say... that we would become soft and cushy. But that's not what it means to live your passion, listen to your heart and soul! Actually, it's with heart and soul that we make clear convictions that are founded in Truth, and contribute to life in a profound and meaningful way. Your passion and clarity of purpose can serve you by clearing the path — or lighting the way as you move forward, unless you give way to fear, judgment or doubt.

This is what happened with the woman at the party. Her judgment almost immediately became discouragement. As I said, she changed right before my eyes. I've seen it before. Suzanne went from passion and excitement about her own authentic, creative expression — to thoughts that led to fear and discouragement.

Did she think that if everyone lived their lives in accord with their authentic expression that perhaps all anyone would want to do is paint? Maybe. But that's not how it works! Or maybe she thought that to follow your Soul Desire would mean you'd be unwilling, unable to look at the difficult situations that require attention. That's not how it works either.

Wisdom Key
Soul Desire is your unique key to living a life you love, a life of purpose.

This derailing thought-process is one we've collectively been leaning toward for many centuries, maybe longer: the idea that one must be power-driven, focused and disciplined, denying pleasure and spirit, refusing creativity and passion in order to succeed. That may have been true, once upon a time, and only some of it is Truth. I believe Suzanne, like I so many times, and maybe you, lumped a bunch of thoughts (veils) together that are now only connected through fear and habit. A bunch of inner wires crossed, causing a short circuit.

All of the possible outcomes from this outdated thought-process are undesirable: discouragement, more fear, no new ideas, disappointment, more effort, stronger polarities with opposing views. The list is longer, but that's enough to make my point. It doesn't have to be like that.

Soul Desire is Your Unique Key...to living a life you love, a life of purpose.

Not by Omission

One more thing about Soul Desire: Clarifying what you do not want does NOT bring you closer to what you want. All it does is focus your light on what you don't want. As with the woman I mentioned earlier, I've heard from many clients and students that they thought if they described what they didn't want, that it would lead them to what they want by omission. Uh, no. All that does is give you a false experience that you are focusing on your desire, and leads to disappointment and frustration and worse. Feel for your Soul Desire.

Desire can be for anything: spiritual, relational, emotional, physical, financial, professional, experiential and so much more. As you allow your desire to emerge from within or be reflected to you, you may find surprises.

Personally, I have been guided to discover Soul Desire by the resonance I found in:

a dream,
a magazine article,
an Italian designer gold bracelet,
looking into the eyes of someone I just met,
a song,
the horizon,
watching a movie,
something I wrote in a journal or
experienced in a dance.

There is no *one* way to discover — or uncover — Soul Desire.

THE SACRED TRUTH OF LOVE

Love Is.

And yet one word frees us of all the weight and pain in life. That word is Love.
— Sophocles

How could words ever express the full scope of what I mean when I speak of Love? Beyond definition, the energy of Love is everywhere and nowhere, all the time for infinity. It is your breath. It is your blood, the beating of your heart when you feel nervous or delighted, sad or enraged. Love is the horizon, a storm, the changing Earth, the night sky.

Love is beaming from your own heart, illuminating everything and everyone around. It is in the glance or hug or smile or tear of every living being.

Expressions of Love are wherever you are, and everywhere you are not.

Love is the source-essence of all creation.
Love is the essence of you.

You are the essence of Love.
You are Love, always and forever.

Love is one energy with limitless expressions. At one point in time you may have known this Sacred Truth in every fiber of your being. Somewhere along the way, since the miracle of your birth or perhaps even before then, you — like most everyone — forgot that you are Love. You became identified with the stuff-ness of your life — what you heard, saw, felt, thought and your reactions to your environment and observations.

Wisdom Key
Love is One Energy with Limitless Expressions.

Before you had reason or understanding, you experienced the energetic, vibrational beliefs of those around you, and their ideas of life and love. Unconsciously you began to don veils — lies, illusions — that kept you separate from your own essence. As you looked out at the world — everyone around you was wearing veils too. We all began to share our veils with each other and they multiplied.

Veiled, we agreed to distortions of love, long-lasting stories of how love leads to loss and betrayal; and how if we open to love, we have to feel grief or pain; or that in order to acquire love, we have to look, do, speak, live, perform to arbitrary standards. The biggest lie of them all: Love comes from other people. To get them to give it to you, you have to earn it.

Everyone agreed. "That's just the way it is," we all said, speaking through our veils of lies.

Awakening to Love

One of my sacred teachers is the ocean. Standing near the edge of the Mendocino bluffs in Northern California, I looked out at the ocean, her massive body before me extended as far as my eyes could see. That's where she met the sky, hazy, gray and bright. It too stretched far and wide, and reached all the way back to me and beyond. In that moment I experienced the horizon. I didn't just see it. I experienced it — a wide, gentle arc where the ocean's reach meets the heavens, which, in turn, caress the edges of the earth. I was in the midst of a kiss between earth and sky; the most tender, ecstatic, eternal kiss.

In that moment I knew in the core of my being that Love is the Source of all creation. I knew that Love was in me, of me, and always surrounding me. It wasn't personal to me, and it was very personal.

Love is cosmic, heavenly, earthly, Godly. It's also palpable, persistent, and transformative. Love is the mother of compassion and forgiveness. Love heals, nourishes, nurtures, and reveals beauty all around. Love radiates from the heart of the universe and from my heart, emanating in all directions.

When a heart opens, Love changes all thought, actions, possibilities. The work is to return to the Heart, to remember and dance in humanly divine expressions of Love.

Wisdom Key
Love is the Source-Essence of all Creation.

I made a private vow that day. I committed myself, a devoted student, to Love. I didn't have the language around it yet. I couldn't say that it was "Love" that I was committed to. That came through my studies and experiences over time.

I am profoundly grateful for that moment, for the awakening that set me on the course to live my Soul's Divine Purpose — and for whatever it was in me that knew to make a sacred vow. That was not something I knew about, consciously, yet I knew in my bones that I must. (We know sacred practices and rituals on a cellular level even if we have not had the influence of them in our outer lives. Perhaps this is an expression of how we are connected to all humanity through all time.)

I had been living my life under a veil formed by an unspoken, unconscious commitment to believing I was essentially unlovable. I bore the weight of this unconscious lie while rejecting this most exquisite Truth: I am a gift of Love. We are, each of us, the essence of love.

Love is in you and of you. With it you can dissolve falsehoods and veils that prevent you from seeing clearly the radiance of your own soul — and the world around you. Open your heart from within so that you may experience the purest joys imaginable — and more.

Love to the Power of Four

In the years that followed that exquisite moment on the ocean's edge, I studied and taught, experienced and embodied lessons of Love that continue to transform my life, and lives of those I touch. One essential lesson came through a vision in meditation.

The vision was of four interlocking petals or leaves, forming a starburst: a mandala of four. I was seated in a spacious temple, light streaming through the pattern in the glass ceiling. I looked up — in my mind's eye — seeing the mandala for the first time. Before closing my meditation I saw the image was duplicated in a mosaic on the temple floor.

Wisdom Key

Love penetrates and permeates all of life.

Captivated by its symmetry and detail, I sat for hours drawing the four nearly identical, interweaving leaves of the mandala. For an entire day and into the night, I drew, replicating the shapes and colors with a magnificent collection of colored pencils. I learned as I drew, marveling at the power of the number four. Often referred to as the fourth chakra, the Heart Chakra awakens unconditional love, the healing presence, balance, radiant compassion and wholeness. There is a stillness in the center from which all things emanate, providing a balance point where there is no struggle in duality. My entire being, mind, body and emotions were filled with the innate knowing this image brought to my awareness.

As I drew, I felt informed — seeing the interwoven qualities of Love, radiating from a center point, pulsing into the center and out beyond the boundaries, revealing four powers of Love. These four powers of Love touch every part of our lives, and are inter-related. So, as you experience Love in any way, you can expand the Love you feel to any and every area of your life. The four powers are:

Divine Love
Self Love
Loving and Being Loved
Spreading Love Around the World

The framed mandala of four hangs on the wall of my office — next to my desk, reminding me that I am, as are we all, connected to infinite wealth and wisdom, that love penetrates and permeates all of life: that we are each whole and part of the whole.

1st Power of Love: Divine Love

Divine Love is pure, Source-Essence of all creation. Divine Love is beyond feeling or sensation, beyond emotion or thought. This essential quality of Love is not out there somewhere, and it is everywhere. You are not — and can never be — separate from Love, yet somehow that is exactly the quality that can make it seem elusive.

All expressions of Love are rivers fed from this original source, Divine Love.

Divine Love can be experienced in church, on sacred lands, in nature, during meditation, through trance dancing, in prayer and meditation. In those exquisite moments when you truly experience the meaning of "Namaste," the Sanskrit word that means, "I bow to you." The deeper meaning is essentially: "that which is the Divine light within me, bows to that which is the Divine light in you."

Wisdom Key

All expressions of Love are rivers fed from the original source: Divine Love.

Pam, one of my dear, long-time friends, once said to me, "This is how I know God exists." We were touring a fine art museum in Washington DC. Pam exemplifies what it means to appreciate art. For her, the miracle of life is reflected in fine art. Together, we stood, gazing into the face of a woman who lived hundreds of years ago in another part of the world, imagining the life she lived.

When Pam said this to me I did not understand her. I had not yet integrated this Sacred Truth into my life. I wasn't willing to accept that miracles of existence had anything to do with God, God's Love, the Universe, Source, Spirit — or any form of Divine expression. It doesn't matter that we agree on a language for this expression. How we relate to the miracle of our lives is unique to each of us. This Sacred

Truth : Love Is, invites us to find our own experience and expression of Divine Love.

As Pam told me that day at the Smithsonian, Divine Love can be experienced and expressed through art. If you have been moved in a deep and spiritual way by art, music, poetry or dance, you know this well. Divine Love is often experienced in ritual and in epiphanies. The life-changing moment I had on the edge of the ocean introduced me to a conscious engagement with Divine Love, long before I had words to say what it was.

You are fully and forever loved by Source. You cannot be separated, except by the illusions created by the veils you don.

2nd Power of Love: Self Love

As Divine Love is big, far-reaching and eternal, Self Love tends to be felt in more intimate, private and often challenging ways. Long before I found the courage and inner fortitude to sustain Self-Love, I practiced seeing myself and my life through the lens of the Divine Love, as if through my own eyes I saw what God sees. Divine Love could see me without all the filters or veils that I'd become accustomed to.

Self Love is no more conditional than Divine Love. There is no measure you must achieve before you qualify to be loved, lovable or loving. You don't have to lose weight or earn a profit, you don't have to have your make-up on, or chauffeur your kids to prove you're worthy of love. You don't even have to overcome shame, repent, or forgive. There is no "doing" to be done.

We learned to resist loving ourselves. "They" said it would be selfish, egotistical, and wicked. Ah, but they, too, were hiding their light, judging, ashamed, or suspicious of love.

It is our highest human calling to love the extraordinary gift of our lives. We cannot meet our potential if we deny ourselves Love.

The mistake so many of us make is that we think that Love is limited, that it comes from other people, and that we have to earn it. Thinking that Love comes from another is the cause of much unnecessary pain. Of course, we want loving connection, companionship and commitment. Our lives are enriched by meaningful relationships and momentary exchanges. Remember: Love is One Energy with Limitless Expressions. There is no one out there who can give it to you, nor take it away. Love is in you, and of you. If you think someone else is keeping you from Love, then you must in some way be keeping yourself from it.

Love is limitless and has simple rules:

Allow Love to flow,
Allow Love to contribute,
Allow Love to heal, enlighten and inform.

Wisdom Key

It is our highest human calling to love the extraordinary gift of our lives.

Want more Love in your life? Begin with yourself. Where are you resisting Love? How could you allow Love to flow freely?... to contribute to your WellBeing?... to heal, enlighten and inform you? Begin within.

We say, "I'll love my body when it's fitter, leaner, stronger, healthier." Or "I'll fall in love with my life when it's the life I want — who would want to love this?" How do you love your brilliance, your circumstances, your history, your dreams if they aren't yet satisfying to you?

You choose love. It's that simple: Choose Love.

Choose to love whom you see when you look in the mirror.

Choose to love the one who hears what you say about yourself, and the one who's talking.

Choose to love now, this moment, exactly as it is.

Choose to love the experiences of your past, the joyous memories, and the hurts, challenges and trials. Infuse your memories and resistances with Love; they will change in character and meaning.

Choose to love yourself when you fail, when you struggle, when you feel an urge to fight, flee or freeze. Even more than that, love that you fail, love the failure itself.

Choose to channel Love anywhere and everywhere.

Infuse love into food as you prepare, serve and eat it.

Place your hands at your heart, and imagine that it grows radiant and full, filling your every cell of your being with the healing qualities of Love.

Love is already here, right where you are. Love yourself for who and how you are in this moment. Love what is.

Choose Love.

These are just a sampling of how simple the practices of Self Love truly are. If you are not experiencing love for yourself, then you are rejecting or resisting it in some way. Unearthing hidden, unconscious resistance frees you to experience even greater Love. Shadow work — the practice of uncovering unconscious commitments you've made to yourself — is an act of Love. Love is what emerges from the depths of your being when your personal truth is brought to light.

Wisdom Key

Love invites you to expose your Soul, your full, authentic, radiant Self.

3rd Power of Love: Loving and Being Loved

Most people consider this expression of Love to be romantic, endearing, intimate, passionate love. They long for it, over and above Divine Love or Self Love. One woman I met last year said to me, somewhat jokingly, "Sure Tambra, communing with God is great and all that, but let's face it, we all want a lover, a partner to share our lives with. We all want to be cherished, appreciated and showered with love by someone desirable." Hmm, I wonder, is that what we really want?

Love is one energy with limitless expressions. You are not limited to experiencing Love only in narrow streams, unless you perceive you are. Putting one expression of Love above any others limits your access to all Love. Love doesn't move in stair-steps, or in linear ways. You don't become worthy or deserving of Love. The energy of Love moves in all directions at all times.

As a former self-defined unlovable, I could tell you endless stories of how love can go wrong, love hurts, love gives someone power over you, and other such sad (untrue) tales. But none of that was — or is — Love. We have allowed the stories we've been told, what we observed through our families and cultures, in movies and fairy tales to cover us with illusions of love that continue to deter us from the joys of authentic connection.

If you long for love and intimacy with other people — and believe you don't have these experiences in your life, ask, yourself, "How am I loving? How do I love myself?

How do I love others? When someone expresses love for me, how do I respond?"

Wisdom Key

Unearthing hidden, unconscious resistance frees you to experience even greater Love.

Loving and Being Loved can feel raw and vulnerable. This power of Love can be very personal, inviting you to expose your Soul, your full, authentic, radiant self. Any veils you have been wearing that say, "No, don't see me." Or "Love hurts," will stir up discomfort — until you release those veils. And the best way to release them: Step into the energy of Love!

I was going around saying to myself, and to my journal: I long for intimacy. I imagined what would be possible when two people connect on a soul-level. I wanted to experience conscious love and connection. I was longing for intimate connection with another person. The trouble was, I had a low tolerance for intimacy. My unspoken, unconscious commitments (of being unlovable) controlled how much intimacy I would allow and with whom: a little at a time with select people, a friend or a lover. I would tolerate a small amount of revealing myself to another. Then I would be so uncomfortable I could no longer be present to them or to myself. Any meaningful connection would just dissolve in that moment. (This tells you a bit about what is was like to be in a relationship with me then.)

One day I suddenly realized that my mother had been extending a loving, generous hand to me, inviting the connection I was longing for. As long as I had been feeling this desire, my beautiful mother had been inviting me to meet her there. I refused her for years — perhaps my whole life — until that day.

Exactly what I wanted was right there in front of me, but I didn't recognize it. I had desire, and an idea of how I would feel when I, if I, ever experienced this kind of love. But I didn't realize that I needed to move through the internal barriers that kept me from it. So I rejected my mother's invitations to meet in the world I dreamed of.

In the back of my mind I may have thought, "Well, I want it, but not with her... Someone else." But she was there, offering to be my guide into unfamiliarity, the place beyond my comfort and unconscious commitments.

Right then and there, sitting at my desk in my San Francisco apartment, I picked up the phone and called my mother. Uncharacteristically, I told her what I'd just realized. I apologized for refusing her. I appreciated her for all the ways she had continued to extend herself to me, inviting me to experience just what I was privately yearning for. This was the most intimate conversation we ever had up till then. We each released veils as we opened our hearts and our voices. We cried, and I'm sure I shook with that body sensation that comes on me when I am being true to my Soul. On that autumn day, many years ago, my mother and I mended a chasm that had been between us. Loving and Being Loved had new expression in my life.

Our relationship continues to grow more intimate and celebratory to this day. We are each other's champions, friends and beloveds.

Wisdom Key

Love First. Love Fully.

"Looking for Love" implies it is not already here. If you desire more Love — for or of another, begin by Being Love. Love first. Love fully. Open to being loved. Celebrate the expressions of Love you have in your life, and those you witness. It is said: "Energy is contagious," which means that the strongest, most persistent energy in your environment spreads and influences all around.

Perhaps you have opened your heart in full appreciation for another, seeing them for who they truly are, radiant and with great potential. Love doesn't require direct reciprocity, yet when it is felt and expressed between two people — that can be one of the most exquisite moments of bliss imaginable and shared.

Loving another does not require or even suggest that the other will Love you in return. Being Loved by another also does not require that you Love them in the same way. Love is not an exchange, rather it is a gift and a way of Being.

Imagine this: You encounter another person — or an animal, or any other living being — and before you extend yourself to engage, you *sense* your connection with them. You are present to yourself, and perhaps through imagination, you sense that beneath you are the roots of your being, under the earth. Your roots extend, as do the roots of the other. You are connected, related, communicating as living beings first. Then, as you are inspired to, you speak.

Lee Glickstein was leading a Speaking Circle I attended to experience for myself what Lee calls Relational Presence. He introduced this image of a web of roots under the earth, connecting us to one another, to the group before each participant was invited to stand at the front of the room and practice. Lee first developed this technique out of a desire to overcome crippling stage fright. What he discovered through the practice not only calmed his nerves, but also led him to facilitate others to connect in a way that is authentic, energetic and intimate.

Speaking Circles International sets in motion a movement that spans far wider than those who want to get over their nerves when public speaking. Relational Presence is an activation of Loving and Being Loved, connecting from your centered self with the humanity of another. I believe this is the same connection you can create with any living being, whether a pet, a forest, a coral reef, or a creature of the sea, earth or air.

Loving another does not *have* to be a living thing. You can Love in this manner: your home, the moon or a piece of music. The experience of Loving does not know the bounds of you and me.

My goal here is to inspire you to Love, to ground your relationships, all your relationships, in Love.

Every experience you have is a reflection of how you are seeing the world, a mirror of your inner landscape. If the Loved One has not appeared in your life, soulfully engage with the Loved One within. Be open to the mysteries: they will inform you and guide you in unexpected ways. For example, if you long for a lover, a partner, a spouse, a best friend, and you are not currently in the relationship you desire, look to your dreams.

Your dreams are messages from your soul. They can reveal the inner dance of your masculine self and your feminine self. There, in the subtlety of dreams and fantasies, so much can be revealed.

Expressions of Loving and Being Loved are limitless...

Conversations — especially with "relational presence"
Creative endeavors in partnership
Feeling your appreciation of another and expressing to them
A heart-felt hug
Giving gifts from your heart
Allowing another to be generous with you
Passionate, present, engaging sexual contact
Holding hands
Collaborating on a project
Listening, openly, curiously
Drawing pictures with a child
Planting a garden together
Saying "Thank you"
Receiving adoration, praise, acknowledgement
Selling your services to an ideal client
Compassionately letting another know you see them
Laughing together
Shaking hands while looking into the eyes of another
Celebrating another's success
Volunteering at a hospice

Offering to help
Tantric practice
Saying "No" when that is your honest response
Preparing a meal for another — or together
Swimming side by side in the ocean
A present, engaging, intentional, mutual kiss
Telling the truth
Raising your glass in a toast
Dancing together
Playing with a pet
Believing in another's potential, in his or her highest calling
Seeking to understand
Releasing any need that the other do, be, feel or have something
Sending a card
And, of course, feeling and saying "I love you."

4th Power of Love: Spreading Love Around the World

Some of my favorite films are based on the true stories of people who have used their life forces to fuel incredible acts of Love and generosity and creative expression. A sampling of such films includes *Ghandi, Paradise Road, Gorillas in the Mist, Milk,* and more recently, *This Is It.* In the recordings of Michael Jackson's final days, it's clear that he loved with great intention and awareness. He knew his music and this concert had one primary mission, one of Spreading Love.

The stories of countless people who, throughout time, have embodied this enactment of Love teach us profound lessons of selflessness, generosity, and interpretations of the Golden Rule. No matter how many of these stories have been told, there are more to tell, and even more we have the opportunity to write today. We will, perhaps, not all be as global or glorious in our offerings, but that in no way lessens the power we each have to Spread Love Around the World. We can broadcast Love through our action, participation and leadership with our families, neighborhoods, communities, churches, schools, businesses, countries, and beyond.

Wisdom Key

Broadcast Love through your action, participation and leadership.

And not just to people. Our Love can be in service to animals and other creatures, to the forests, oceans, to the planet, or perhaps even to the cosmos. Each of us is unique in how we choose to serve, aid, support and facilitate the WellBeing of others with open hearts and minds.

I am drawn to the image of concentric circles; a centering image of ripples in water, radiating out from the original source... perhaps where someone dropped a pebble in the stillness. Spreading Love Around the World feels like ripples that move beyond your initial actions — that first pebble — touching those whom you serve, who in turn affect another, then another and another.

Tambra Harck

Ripples touched me when I met Don, Linda and Coco, and first heard them tell their interwoven tale of service, the thousands of lives they touch every day. A successful self-made businessman, Don Smith wanted some time to himself after he retired to pursue his passion for sailing. He honored his desire as he sailed the Caribbean and other parts of the world, loving the open water and the joys of sailing. Yet, after a few months he started to feel restless and bored.

Throughout most of his adult life Don had been actively contributing to the WellBeing of others — so I guess it was in character for him to leave the Mediterranean and head down to Malawi, Africa at the request of a friend.

Don says of his first visit to the villages in this small African country, "I could see they were hungry. I could see their poverty. I also knew there was no way I can come into a foreign country — I'd never even been to Africa before — and start telling people how they ought to live their lives. That won't work. I don't even understand their problems thoroughly."

Wisdom Key

Love ripples out from a single act, reaching corners of the earth you may not even imagine exist.

He decided that the only way he could really know if he wanted to help was to go there and live. So he went to Malawi to rent a house in the city of Blantyre. He met Linda Limbe. She showed houses for a law firm that handled rental properties. As the two drove around, touring rentals, Don learned more about Africa and the villages from Linda. They developed a friendship. Soon, she volunteered to accompany him as his translator as he began to work with the village men. Don was drawn to work with the men to develop irrigation systems. But he saw that the women had more potential.

Even though Malawi women do not usually get to go to school, or even learn to read and write, Don says, "They have a positive attitude... They wanted things to change. They were like children in their thirst for learning. And they didn't just listen, they would act on it." Lessons in sanitation and about diet quickly improved the health and safety of families.

Don brought Linda to the United States for a few days to demonstrate the essence of what they're doing in Malawi. Synchronicity was at play — I had spontaneously decided to attend this conference myself. Linda and I were standing together in a buzzing room, filled with a few hundred people, all of them talking. For a long, timeless, silent moment, she and I held hands, as I honored her for the grace and generosity with which she lives her life. I can still see her bright eyes, looking into mine. She loves people and sees the potential in them to create and grow and contribute to their own WellBeing, and to those around them.

A beautiful, big-hearted woman, Linda grew up in a poor village. With good parents and a lot of hard work, she was able to complete her education and earn a Bachelor's degree. She suggested to Don that she could teach a few of the women to read. Don knew from his years in business that they could also teach the women to make a little income. Instead of micro-loans or welfare, the non profit organization Village Empowerment was formed, thus gives a village the money needed to start a Women's Club. The club asks a church for space to meet. In turn, they do some work in the church, repairing a roof, for instance. There is an exchange, an offering made in reciprocity. This is one of the many ways that the energy of Love is spreading through these villages.

Wisdom Key

Generosity of heart knows no bounds.

The women of the village come together three days a week to read and write, to sew and knit, making garments to sell in the market, and to learn to start and run businesses. I am told they sing and laugh when they gather!

They provide a day care for orphans of the village. These children are usually seen as a burden, unwanted by family members who themselves are struggling to survive. In the day care, these children are cared for and fed. The Women's Club also serves elderly and handicapped members of the village, providing them food and attention, even cleaning their homes. This early system worked well, but there was still more that could be done. Which is another way of saying: There was more Love to Spread!

When a new village requests the organization come in to help them build a sustainable community, they go to the *Village Headman*, a person you might think of as a chief. About half the *Headmen* are women. Don says they are nice people who care about the welfare of those in their villages. A request is made for the use of a piece of land — perhaps for a garden where they will grow food for the orphans. The request is always granted. The women plant and tend the garden. Their crops produce enough to feed the children in the day care, and to sell in the market for a little profit.

Serving food with Love and appreciation is a fundamental and ancient expression of Spreading Love. You may choose to bring a meal to a neighbor, feed those in your community who are hungry or homeless, or serve a meal for your family. I invite you to offer sustenance with awareness and generosity of spirit — maybe even sing while you prepare it!

Wisdom Key

Whatever you do, wherever you go,
there is Love to spread around.

Here's how the Village Empowerment system works: A neighboring village in Malawi — or in surrounding countries — sees what is happening and wants the same thing for themselves, Don encourages an established village to help the new one. There's no initial loan to pay back. Don's view is, "...pay it back by helping your neighbor. There were 34 villages established when I spoke to Don in the summer of 2009, mostly in Malawi, plus more than 200 requests from villages in countries throughout Africa that want to start their own empowerment programs.

Linda works with the women. Now on staff as Program Director, she speaks with such love and respect for the women and children she serves. Many people are overwhelmed by the need of others. Linda shows us how to be both a generous spirit and to take inspired actions.

As the ripples spread from village, so to they spread when Coco met Don. He inspired her, too, in, "his audacity to believe that he can make a difference." She isn't in Africa, working with the villages. Coco lives in New York. Stories of villages that had transformed into sustainable, prosperous communities inspired her to help. Sure she could write a check, and she did, but it wasn't enough. She saw that she could help articulate the message of what the organization is doing, and start sharing it with the world. (Until this time most of the funds were provided personally by Don.)

Wisdom Key

Have the audacity to believe you can make a difference with your Love ~ then act with conviction and grace.

One expression of Spreading Love Around the World is seen in a growing trend of conscious business. Marketing tactics are usually intentionally manipulative, focusing on your pain. In contrast, the Sacred Truth "Love Is" has begun to seep into business practices and we are starting to see more marketing messages that celebrate possibility and opportunity rather than pain, shame and suffering. Coco chose to speak from this perspective as she helped craft the message for the organization.

She told me, "I see in the women who live in the villages the presence of joy and love and celebration in their lives on a consistent basis. Every day that they gather, they laugh and they sing and they tell stories." To Coco this is robust prosperity. As she considered ways to share Village Empowerment with people in the US, she chose to infuse the "richness in spirit" that is vital in the villages into the fund- and awareness-raising. Events, called "Prosperity Parties," are hosted in homes across the country. Guests are invited to open their hearts not only to the villagers in Africa, but also to their own lives and the prosperity they experience — and to celebrate.

"We all have different life purposes," Don says, "but we have one life purpose in common — and that is to serve our fellow man in some way or another." That is the underlying message of Spreading Love Around the World.

Whatever you do, wherever you go, there is Love to Spread. Around:

A kind gesture to another.
A charitable donation.
An expression of appreciation.

Leading or joining a team of people who together harness more energy to promote growth, prosperity, wellness, beauty, peace, opportunity — service that contributes to Life. The possibilities for "how" are endless.

Open to Divine Love.
Love Yourself.
Love and Be Loved.
Spread Love Around the World.

THE FIFTH SACRED TRUTH

You Are Not Your Veils.

Our thoughts, our words, and deeds are the threads of the net we throw around ourselves.
— Swami Vivekanada

If the Beautiful One is not inside you, then what is that light hidden under your cloak?
— Jalal ad-Din Rumi

You are a radiant soul, infinite and powerful. Any way in which you reject, deny, resist or forget that you are a radiant soul, infinite and powerful, is a veil — an untruth, a lie, an unconscious commitment.

You are an infinite and powerful being with unlimited capacity for experiencing and participating in life in profound and joyous ways. Your Soul's Divine Purpose can only be lived by you. Your Soul Desire can only be expressed by you. Only you can be the channel of Love that you are uniquely capable of being.

You are not your thoughts, feelings or sensations, your stories or circumstances. You are not a product of your history or your memories. This Sacred Truth, in a direct way, says "Stop trying to be what you're not." This is not an affirmation. It's a wake-up call, inviting you to release that which binds you to thinking small, shrinking away from your magnificence, believing in any way that you don't matter.

There is a profound difference between having a thought and being that thought. You experience thoughts and emotions. You experience sensations. They do not define you. You experience memories and fantasies, ideas and intuitions. None of these experiences define you. When you identify with what you're not, you disconnect from — or resist — the magnificent being that you are. Then you find yourself swimming — more likely drowning — in the energy of what you're not. Your veils limit your understanding and ability to interpret and be entertained by all the yummy, wondrousness that you are capable of being.

Wisdom Key

There is a profound difference between having a thought and being that thought.

You may think you are your thoughts, and that without your thoughts you wouldn't exist. Those are your thoughts thinking that. Maybe you are identified with your feelings or emotions — and you feel that without them you wouldn't exist. Many people believe they are a product of their upbringing, their environment, their ancestry and so on. Our compulsions to identify with our thoughts, feelings and sensations, stories and circumstances, all create heavy, clingy burdens. It's no wonder that for millennia people have been seeking to feel better emotionally, physically, mentally, spiritually and relationally!

Of course we want to feel better! We've been so identified with our veils of illusions that our collective and individual longings to live glorious, meaningful, and joyous lives are a constant pressure, urging us to unveil and really *live* our lives.

An example of how our veils can seem real, and propel us into unintended outcomes, is seen in the story of Rachel* who told me during a private consultation, "Success is the best revenge." Ouch. This thought led to a series of other thoughts and then actions that were all motivated by the idea of revenge. When she came to work with me she was in the midst of a major life transition. In the past year she'd lost two properties to foreclosure. Her business was floundering and she was generally unhappy and unhealthy. Then her 11-year relationship ended suddenly. Her impulse to create new successes right away was a way to get back at him for leaving her. Again: Ouch!

Wisdom Key

Slight and subtle shifts often create deep, lasting change.

As we worked together, Rachel saw that her thought, "Success is the best revenge" was just that: a thought. She

* Some names have been changed to honor privacy.

saw that if she acted with this thought as her motivation, anything she created would be infused with the energy of revenge. Removing the thought-veil involved redefining success. She released herself from being an agent of revenge — during our call — and began to find inspiration for creating a life she loved. Energy shifts can be subtle and slight, while creating deep, lasting change. Now she's in love with what she's creating! You see, it doesn't take time to stop trying to be what you're not. You simply stop.

If We Deeply Understood

In the study of business marketing, one of the first things you learn is to identify your customers' pain — and then how to lead them into that pain till it intensifies. Then you learn how to show them that you have the solution to ending their pain.

I believe that if we, all of humankind, deeply, in an integrated, whole way, understood that we are not our pain, we would redefine how business is done. Businesses would speak to potential and possibility and emerge from the old model of restricted supply and demand and the perspective of control and market share, to growing and expanding because they are serving the greater good of their customers. As a buyer, you would choose to invest in, support and appreciate the companies that reflected your highest good. Your buying power would align your actions with your Soul Desire.

Your relationships, too, would change completely, if you deeply understood that you are not your thoughts, feelings or sensations, stories or circumstances. You would no longer choose who to be with, how to act, what to expect or accept based on fear or comfort or acquiescence, or whatever unconscious motivations might have been at play before.

Wisdom Key

Unveil to your radiance, power and grace.

Instead, imagine this:

> Imagine in your relationships you unveil your radiance, your power and your grace. Imagine that you see the people in your life through eyes of the infinite being that you are, not from how "they make you feel," nor by what you get from them. You learn and grow and delight in yourself and in each other.

If you deeply understood that you are not your thoughts, feelings, sensations, your stories or your circumstances, you would have compassion and practice forgiveness as a way of being, rather than something you do. You would ask for what you want, not what you think you can get, or what you deserve. You would celebrate the achievement, success, opportunity and joy of others... and you would know that their having more doesn't mean you have less. You would be forthcoming when you made a mistake.

As a spiritual seeker, if you deeply understood that while your thoughts, stories, self-induced limits or burdens may have served you at one time, they are not the only ways to experience safety, security, value, or to propel you to grow. Sure, you can learn and grow from the pain and struggle that comes with *what you're not*. So, too, can you grow by embracing who you are. The latter is much more fun! *Who you are* will shine your light into the shadowy recesses of your resistance, and issue you into more of your Self more quickly, with more ease and more joy than your veils ever have.

What Are They?

Are you now asking, "If my thoughts, feelings and sensations, stories and circumstances are not me, then what are they?" Simply, they are transmitters of information — as are your intuition, insight and instincts. They give you access to information, seen and unseen, tangible and intangible, material and mystical. We are each one of us intricate, information highways with constant input from unlimited inner and outer sources. In an attempt to grapple with all that input, we each developed a unique combination of filters.

As I see it, each of us has a few filters that we keep open, while we perceive that others don't exist. A man I mentored with years ago has a keen mind (and used to identify himself as his thoughts). While he had honed psychic sensitivities through his spiritual practices, he did not have an experience of being intuitive. He used to ask for my intuitive read on situations, trusting that I had natural access to it. I didn't realize how strong my intuition was until he asked me to share with him how I experienced my sense of knowing. That's what I had always said, "I just know." Before that I was identified with "my knowing," just as he had been identified with his thoughts.

What I learned from my mentoring friend was that we each have innate gifts and abilities to interpret the information that we have access to, and that we can develop skills in other approaches. I have honed my innate skills in intuition, reading patterns and storytelling, while I continue to develop emotional authenticity, sharing my inner process, and intentional thought.

Wisdom Key

Sacred Truths invite you more fully into the miracle of creation.

Your thoughts, feelings, sensations, your history — like your stories, memories, justifications, and your circumstances are all simply filters. You can use these filters to gain awareness, to observe yourself and to discover veils of untruths that you've been hiding under. You can choose how and if you want to respond. If you feel imprisoned by your thoughts, shackled by your feelings, or punished by your body, you are looking at the veils that prevent you from seeing, being, and loving this miracle of existence.

The preceding Sacred Truths each invite you more fully into the miracle of creation. As you create a new or expanded reality — a richer, joyous experience, the magnetic pull of history and habit will tug at you, trying to bring you back to the familiar, to your former comfort zone — back to defining yourself with limitations rather than embracing your new reality.

Wisdom Key

You can choose to disempower anything that excuses you from living your personal greatness, your Soul's Divine Purpose.

Every time you tell a story about yourself that dismisses your dreams or your ambitions, or demeans your choices or behaviors, you give power to that story, taking energy away from your Soul Desire, channeling it instead into resistance. You have the choice to stop giving your life force over to your veils. You can choose to disempower anything that excuses you from living your personal greatness, your Soul's Divine Purpose. Not through rejection of them, but rather by channeling your energy into your Purpose, your Desire, your connection to your essence.

The lesson of this Sacred Truth is: *Be who you truly are.*

When my Soul's Divine Purpose was first revealed to me in very specific terms, I resisted it. I knew deep within that it was true for me, yet thoughts I clung to sounded something like this: "Who am I to help people transcend from a perpetual state of suffering? I gain my strength and perseverance from suffering! I feel shackled by my own inability to get out of this rut. I don't want to be seen by so many people! They will judge me as being a fraud. How could I be trustworthy as a teacher-mentor when I haven't mastered the very things I'm supposed to be teaching? What if I do it just a little?" yada yada.

Wisdom Key

Be who you truly are.

A life-long learner, I was driven by a force I didn't always understand. I was compelled to learn and grow while hoping that I would one day wake up with a sense of freedom and WellBeing; that I would get out of my own way so that I could share my gifts and awaken others to theirs. To be honest, my spiritual exploration and my self-development were, for years, an attempt to fix "what's wrong with me." In all my efforts, I clung to the veils that would have me deny my own beauty and resist living in a state of grace. I was unwilling to accept that I truly am a radiant, exquisite and generous being. Mine was a classic, sad-n-sorry tale of living in the hazy world of *what you're not!*

You can end struggles. You can allow abundance, joy, love and WellBeing into your life right now. No matter how much or how little you have experienced joy, love, abundance and WellBeing before, they are yours for the experiencing. They are in you and of you! Here and now.

The system is clear:

> When you perpetuate lies (which could take the form of self-doubt, shame, blame, fear, illness, injury, what someone said or did to you — yesterday or 40 years ago, fear of being seen, fear of being invisible, or any other lies that keep you from who you are,) you deny your light, your essence, your Purpose, your expression: you deny who you are. You infuse your perceived limitations with your creative power. It's never a pretty picture. Never. Even if you are comfortable, you have a persistent sense of discontent, of living a "less-than life."
>
> AND
>
> When you choose to be who you are, you dispel any lies that mask your beauty, your potential, your radiance or your love. You can redefine and clear away any thoughts, feelings, sensations, stories or circumstances that appear to be in your way. You choose thoughts, feelings, and so on that bring you more fully into your Soul's Divine Expression. Then the expanded thoughts, feelings, insights, stories, etc. feed your Spirit and propel your growth.

Discovering and releasing your veils — whether they are unconscious commitments, lies, thoughts, mistaken beliefs, feelings, ideas, stories or in other forms — is profoundly empowering, frightening, liberating, and disorienting — all at the same time! This leads us to the Sixth Sacred Truth.

THE SIXTH SACRED TRUTH

Believe. Act in Faith. Trust.

Keep on praying for faith because it is through prayer that you develop all your wonderful qualities of soul.
— Myrtle Fillmore

Just trust yourself and you'll learn the art of living.
— Johann Wolfgang Von Goethe

Believe

I delight in exploring the origins of words. In my research I learned that the word *believe* comes from two old English words, *be* and *lifon*. *Be* meaning "life" (as in being), and *lifon*, which means "according to." Older versions of language trace the word back to mean "to hold dear, to love." When you put these derivations together, the message is superbly fitting to everything we are exploring together. The meaning of *believe* is this: Be in Accord with, Hold Dear, Love Life.

Be in accord with love and life! To Believe is a state of being that honors and resonates with Love and Life. Believing is all-powerful, as the state of being I'm talking about is transformative and informative in ways that do not come about through the tried, old methods of doing. When Ghandi said, "You must be the change you want to see in the world," he spoke from this Sacred Truth. He knew that change — true, lasting, change — starts from a state of being.

Wisdom Key

Be in accord with Love and Life.

He didn't say, "Talk about," or "Plan for," or "Demand others..." He said, "*Be* the change." Be, first. Then from your state of Being in Accord with Love and Life, you will be inspired to actions and opportunities that align with your choice to believe.

Believe you can and will be, do, have, experience your Soul Desire, your highest expression. Believe it with all your heart and soul. No questions, no doubt. Absolutely believe. Absolutely BE your essential nature, your radiance.

Act in Faith

In his book, *Callings*, Gregg Levoy wrote, "Beyond a certain point, faith is the magic lamp..." Faith lights your way. Illumination is not enough, though; you must then step in the direction of illumination, and then step again, and again.

There is a greeting card image that I have kept in my office for years. This man is walking on a tightrope, off the edge of a cliff — much like the image you see on the Fool card of a Tarot deck. One end of the rope is behind him, the other in his hand. Each next step requires him to have faith that the rope will be there, suspended, under his feet.

Wisdom Key

Acting in Faith builds the bridge between Believing and Reality.

Whether you see the first step as a tightrope or as a rung along an emerging staircase, Acting in Faith builds the bridge between Believing and Reality.

> Have faith that you are being shown the way, that your Highest Good is being revealed to you.
>
> Take your first step.
>
> Enliven your actions with the energy of Believing.
>
> Be diligent and bold in your actions.

Tambra Harck

Act in accord with your Soul Desire, and with Your Soul's Divine Purpose.

As members of a modern-day mystery school, we came together in sacred space to practice various forms of meditation and energy work, and to engage in deep, mystical studies. One of the meditations we practiced was *Sacred Temple by the Sea*. This meditation was created by Dr. Brugh Joy, a beloved spiritual teacher. Over the years, it was led by many other teachers, therapists and in sacred community.

Sacred Temple by the Sea accesses sacred resources through visualizing and embodied imagination as you approach the sea, calling forth and entering your temple. No one suggests what your temple looks or feels like or where on the sea it might be. Images and sensations come from your imagination, your soul. Often members of our sacred tribe created artistic expressions of their temples through painting, drawing, sculpting.

When we gathered, Jerry* sat in the circle hearing his fellow tribe members speak of their experiences, sharing their artistic renderings of their temples. Yet for years his own meditations revealed no images to him.

One morning, Jerry shared with all of us, "I saw my temple. This is the first time I saw it. I have followed the map for this meditation for over four years — I never once saw an image — until today." He marveled at his new experience,

---

* Some names have been changed to honor privacy.

describing his visual and visceral imagery. It was a tender moment to witness.

Imagery isn't necessary — not even the goal — although with this meditation, it can deepen your experience. My guess is that he sat to do *Sacred Temple by the Sea* several hundred times, never once seeing an image of the sea or a temple. He was Acting in Faith.

Faith is the bridge between Believing and New Reality. Jerry traversed his bridge at least once a week for four years before he had any visual indication that there even was a bridge!

Wisdom Key

Be diligent in your actions as you act in faith.

Jerry's story shows us an important aspect of Acting in Faith: discipline. The root of the word *discipline* is, of course, "disciple" which means *pupil*. Jerry was a dedicated student, committed to taking a step — repeatedly, as necessary. When you Act in Faith, you take a step, then you take the next step, and the next, for as long as there are steps appearing before you... even when you don't know that there is a step beyond the one you are taking.

Doug had a feeling that he had to make a change. His job at the airport paid well, and gave him great benefits and job security. Yet, the feeling kept at him, nagging at him to get out. Living in San Francisco, he was meeting people who were starting their own businesses and doing well. They were an inspiration to him. He wanted to see what he could create, but he was afraid to leave his job.

When he finally decided it was time, he told his friends and co-workers that he had given notice. They panicked. "Come on, man, what are you doing? How are you gonna make this kind of money? You're giving up a sure thing here!" He knew their concerns were genuine, but he was committed to following his instinct, even if it went against convention. A year earlier, Doug started a little business on the side. Somehow that gave him courage to take the next step. He had dreams, ideas and opportunities that he knew he couldn't or wouldn't pursue as long as he had the cushion of his job.

Even though they didn't understand or agree with his decision, his friends threw a party to wish him well on his last day at work. Doug left the airport, heading home from that era of his life for the last time. He merged onto the freeway and in a moment he was overwhelmed. He was unable to see, not sure where he was. He managed to pull his car to the shoulder, and sat behind the wheel in tears. He felt lost.

As he remembers that day more than 25 years ago, he describes it as a turning point, his biggest leap of faith. Martin Luther King, Jr. is reported to have said, "Take the first step in faith. You don't have to see the whole staircase, just take the first step." Well, Doug did just that. He didn't know that his staircase would lead to becoming a successful real estate investor, an importer, an entrepreneur, an inventor, and a man who continually values growth — personal, spiritual, professional growth. He took the first step, the one that was right in front of him. That's the only step any of us can take: the first one from here.

Acting in Faith does not require perpetual motion. You may be guided to take a nap or paint or sit in contemplation or tour the farmers market. Or you may find that the next step is one that feels crazy-making-scary. Having faith — much like courage — does not mean that you will skate through without fear. Moving into a new experience often feels scary, as Doug can tell you, but that is no reason not to follow your magic-faith-lamp.

Wisdom Key

See the light of your own lamp surrounding you. Have faith and take your next step.

Life is simply asking you to grow, to expand into a newer, more evolved expression of yourself. In his spiritual guidebook, *Lessons from the Source*, Jack Armstrong writes, "Faith is the certainty that you are in the universal flow, and that nothing can happen to you that is not for your highest good."

I see the light of your lamp surrounding you: a clear, brilliant aura. Have faith and take your next step.

Trust

Trust begins with being trustworthy with yourself. Self-Trust is essential to your WellBeing. When you honor and align with Sacred Truths, you create Trust in, of and for yourself — and in your connection with Source, the Divine. Self-Trust is built on forgiveness, love, honesty, compassion, kindness, wonder, being true in your words, thoughts, actions and intentions. What do you require to be worthy of your own trust? What do you trust in yourself?

When you bring awareness and intention to being trustworthy, you build greater Trust while you illuminate any areas of your life where you are not aligned, or you are out of integrity.

Wisdom Key

The one person whose trust is essential to your WellBeing is you.

Trusting yourself is...

Nourishing your wholeness with appreciation for your life and who you are.

Continuous, consistent, aligned action that furthers your highest intentions and Soul Desires.

Maintaining integrity, a state of being whole.

Beyond being honest.
Keeping no secrets. Telling no lies.

Trusting yourself is...
Forgiving mistakes or wrongdoings, and consequences you created.
Releasing yourself from the bondage of your past. It's over; let it rest.
Being kind in your self-talk — as kind as you would to another soul who shines their light into the world.
Believing in yourself and your potential, relentlessly.

Trusting yourself is...
Honoring your Soul, your unique expression and your spark of vitality!
Listening to your intuition.
Following your inner guidance — even when it seems contrary to the norm or others' expectations.
Seeking to live your Soul's Divine Purpose every day, in every way.
Following your dreams and your callings all the way through.

Trusting yourself is...
Realizing that you do not have to "go it alone" because Life is not a solo ride.
Allowing yourself to be supported by Life.
Knowing that all you need is available to you in right timing.
Paying attention to opportunities and acting on them as they appear.
Asking for more, better, recognizable opportunities!

Saying, "Yes" when that's the answer in your heart — even when it's scary, unfamiliar, or you don't know how you'll get there.
Knowing that there is power in "No" when that's what's true for you. Then saying it clearly.

Trust that Life has your best interests at heart.
Then show up for it with all you've got!

PART III

A Call to Continue

The Call to Continue

I believe that man will not merely endure: he will prevail. He is immortal, not because he alone among creatures has an inexhaustible voice, but because he has a soul, a spirit capable of compassion and sacrifice and endurance.

— William Faulkner

Around the time I began write to this book I received a message. I was in meditation, preparing for my yoga practice. As this message emerged in my consciousness, I noticed the quality of it and recognized it as something other than a thought. I keep a drawing pad and pencils near my yoga mat for times such as this. I completed my meditation and sprinkled a few colored pencils out of their box so I could draw and write the message of what I've now come to know as the *Energy Channels of Transformation.*

This message has informed much of what I share with you here, and in many ways gave me clarity about the service that this book is intended to provide. This has been an experience of Co-Creation, as I've participated with the mystical and brought it into practical application. I offer you the message too, in hopes that Divine Inspiration will serve you in your journey.

The essence of the message is this:

> *Our most natural state is being **Vitally Awake** each and every moment of our lives. If we are not having that experience, it is because we are rejecting our essential connection to **Divinity** or Source, and/or our **Vitality**, and/or our **Soul Desire**.*

When we forget, reject, deny or resist our innate connection to Source, Vitality or Soul Desire, we experience pain and suffering. We label this suffering with words like loneliness, disappointment, resentment, shame, contempt, doubt, suspicion, unworthiness, hopelessness, desperation or exhaustion. We feel lousy about ourselves or about our lives in some way. We complain, blame, envy. And even though we may try to get out of it, we keep slipping back into the quicksand of an unfulfilling life. If you've been there, you know what it's like to drop into the gravitational pull of that muck.

Then down in the muck, most people say, "I can't have what I want. Why bother trying? I need to get used to this. It's as good as it gets," resigning themselves to a life of mediocrity and disappointment. They set up residence in mediocre-ville. They surround themselves with other people who live there, too. Together, they go along, as one year blurs into the next with occasional highlights and frequent bouts of drama and worry. They feel like the walking dead, but they're too numb to know it. I'm sure you know someone who lives in mediocre-ville. Perhaps that someone is you — even as a part-time resident.

My dear, I want you to know that is not LIVING! *Living*, truly experiencing your life with joy, meaning and love, is very simple. These three Energy Channels of Transformation provide direct, immediate access as you:

- Maintain and nourish your innate connection with the **Divine,** Source-energy, God, the Universe; and
- Feel and express your **Vitality**; and
- Continually experience and resonate with your **Soul Desire**.

Living in this way leads you from mediocre-ville to "Glory, Hallelujah, I Love My Life!"

Does this mean you never face challenges or difficulties? No. Challenges are there to show you where you are holding yourself back — not to hold you back. One day Brenda* called me to say she was ready to finally break free of something that had been holding her back. Four years ago a work relationship ended badly, and no matter what she did to get over it, her hurt and upset would spring back in her face like a jack-in-the-box. She told me about the event and her former business partner's behavior, and hers. She was accountable about her part in creating the drama and what led to the break-up. But that was long over. (Holding on to the past — whether it's happy or upsetting — is not being Vitally Awake! Vitally Awake is here and now.)

* Some names have been changed to honor privacy.

Brenda is smart, highly skilled, has done amazing things in her career and as a result has affected the lives of hundreds of thousands of people in empowering ways. At this point, after four years, she was starting to worry: Was that one event going to put an end to her viable business and future ... because she just couldn't seem to get over it?

It was not the event that caused her years of suffering, but her reaction to the event. This slight shift in her perception lifted her out of the dull, depressed place she'd been living in. I am not exaggerating when I tell you: everything began to change. She had been holding on to her reaction. The tighter she held onto the reaction, the more she would feel hurt, betrayed, dismayed, disempowered, vindictive (and the list goes on.) Addressing any of those feelings kept her in the spin cycle, whirling 'round and 'round, unable to break free.

On this day, during our call, something was different. She was committed to getting out of spin. "This is it. Tambra, I'm ready to shift out of this." The discovery she made was that she had lost her faith. The tighter she held to the upset, the looser her connection to Spirit became until she no longer trusted her Divine essence. Our work together was focused on clearing the Energy Channel of Divinity. The shift happened while we were on the phone, then and there. That's what I mean that sometimes the slightest shift will result in complete transformation.

The Channel of Divinity already exists for each of us, always. It never leaves you. However, as Brenda experienced, you can shut yourself off from it. You can forget that you are an Infinite and Powerful Being. When you do, that's where the suffering seeps in. Remember, reconnect to Source, to your unique experience of Divine essence, and a renewed, fresh sense of wholeness re-emerges.

That's what Brenda experienced. She released the reaction that she'd been gripping hold of and restored her sense of being Infinite, the Creator of her own experience. In an instant everything about the event with her former business partner and the years that followed changed in her perception. She had renewed energy and clarity. Her outlook was fresh and vitalized, and within a few days she started receiving requests from former clients she hadn't heard from in years. Once she opened her Energy Channel of Divinity, her environment and opportunities changed as well, and continue to as I write this, two years later.

When your channels are clear, they are evidenced by ease and grace that you have in any given moment. When you are feeling challenged, frustrated, disappointed, apprehensive, victimized or unable to transcend a situation — those are all indications that an Energy Channel is not clear. The quality of each of the Energy Channels is different; as are the ways you may experience them.

Wisdom Key

Divinity + Vitality + Desire =
an Abundant, Joyous, Meaningful
Life that You Love.

Let's take a look at each of the Channels. I share with you both my personal experiences as well as what I understand to be universal perceptions. For each Energy Channel I show you ways to relate to, attune with and increase your awareness of your experience, as described below:

- **Embodied Expressions** show you ways that you may experience a physical, sensory or imagined sense of the Channels.
- **Perspective** demonstrates the state of being, the words, feelings, statements, ideas or thoughts that may emanate from within you when you are clear and connected with the Channels.
- **Adverse Experiences** describe common behaviors or experiences that indicate when you are not clear and connected with the Channels.
- **Soul-Level Attunements** are suggested practices to guide you to clearing and connecting with the Channels

The Energy Channel of Divinity (Source)

Divinity as Embodied Expression

Tingles, shivers, what one of my client's calls, "Goddess Bumps," these are some of the embodied experiences of an open channel. In many yoga practices, this channel is opened through the sense of your feet on the ground, connected to, tapped into the Earth herself; and through clearing your mind and opening the upper chakras. I often lead meditations that invite you to imagine the energies of heaven and earth, two intertwining, spiraling ribbons of energy that inform and enliven you: body, mind, heart and soul. There is a unique-to-you embodied experience and there are universal experiences.

Perspective of Divinity

Read aloud the following statements and notice the energy of them in your being. These are not affirmations, rather expressions of the *state of being* you may experience when your Energy Channel of Divinity is clear and activated.

Divinity allows me to see through my eyes as God sees, with Love and understanding, compassion and grace.
I feel and know myself to be One with everything and everyone.
I have a sense of belonging.
God, Source, Spirit wants me to be joyous, prosperous, generous.
I see opportunities for joy, love and gratitude throughout each day.
I celebrate the multitude of blessings in my life.
I see, feel and create beauty all around me.
The Universe is friendly to me and only wants the best for me.
I show up as a willing participant in my life.
I participate and partner with Divine Source.
All that is possible for anyone is possible for me.
I willingly sacrifice whatever keeps me from my highest good.
I forgive others and myself easily, releasing any ideas that perpetuate feelings of being wounded or wronged.
I know my life has meaning and purpose.
I live each day honoring that my life has meaning and purpose.
I am supported in the highest way. (Perhaps through other people, synchronicity, intuition, karma, by Divine guidance, willingness or courage)

I have direct and intentional communication with Spirit and with my Soul. (Perhaps through dreams, meditation, prayer, in contemplation, in nature, journaling, gardening, or in dance.)
I am Infinite and Powerful.
I have an intense sense of WellBeing.

Adverse Experiences of Divinity
Signs that you are not experiencing the Energy Channel of Divinity (Source, Spirit, God) as clear and connected include:

Feelings of boredom.
Indecision.
Feeling envious, jealous or covetous.
Self doubt.
Questioning your worthiness, especially of Divine Love or Self Love.
Efforting: trying harder and harder.
Thinking that if someone wins someone else loses.
Looking for validation or approval.
Believing you're on your own.
Being controlling or unsupportable.
Avoiding your sacred practices.
Perceiving that God doesn't love you.
Considering that your life doesn't matter.
Refusing to forgive yourself or others.

Soul-Level Attunements
When you have Adverse Experiences — or if you want to enhance your Energy Channel of Divinity, here are some simple practices to bring you into a higher state of attunement:

Meditate.

Pray with praise. (no poor-poor-pitiful-me prayers)
Set an altar for your sacred practice.
Commune with nature.
Chant. You can use a CD with sacred chants so you have the experience of blending your voice with others in prayerful song.
Begin a "spiritual food" journal. Record the moments when you experience or witness spiritual enrichment.
Once each day ask yourself, "Whom have I closed my heart to today?"
Journal-dialog with the Divine.

Also, look at the Life-Integration Practices for Sacred Truths 1, 4, 5 and 6 for other ways to strengthen your connections to Source/Divinity.

The Energy Channel of Vitality

Vitality as Embodied Expression

Vitality is in, of and around your body. It is the experience of being passionate and present — in your body. There's a vibrancy and awake-ness, but it's not hyper. Imagine what it's like to have a body-felt experience of joy, pure joy, even in stillness.

Perspective of Vitality

Again, perspective is a state of being: the words, feelings, statements, ideas or thoughts that may emanate from within you when you are clear and connected with the Channels.

Read aloud the following statements and notice the energy of them in your being. These are not affirmations, rather expressions of the *state of being* you may experience when your Energy Channel of Vitality is clear and activated.

Vitality is my natural physical and energetic state.
I feel joy in my being.
My body is my beloved.
My body provides me access to great wisdom.
I experience great pleasure through presence.
I celebrate the amazing inner and outer functions of my body.
I see and appreciate the beauty that I am.
I experience joy, love and gratitude throughout each day.
I partner with my body, mind and soul for my highest good, my highest expression.
I honor the power of my mind and focus my thoughts for my highest good.
I forgive myself any transgressions I have made against my body — or in any other way, including moments of ridicule, judgment, comparison, abuse or abandonment.
I value supreme self-care, lovingly nourishing and tending to my body.
I am as an extension of the earth's vitality.
I have direct and intentional communication with the wisdom of my body. (Perhaps through dreams, breathing, sensation, intuition, gesture, in nature, yoga, or in dance.)
My body is the temple of my Soul.
I connect with others who are vital. Together, we are more alive.
I am aware of the stimuli in my environment and choose to be motivated by my own sense of Self rather than by societal, cultural, familial or habitual input.
I have an intense sense of WellBeing in my body and my surroundings.

I am in Love with Life!

Adverse Experiences of Vitality
Signs that you are not experiencing the Energy Channel of Vitality as clear and connected include:

Creating drama in your life.
Behaviors that are dangerous to your WellBeing.
Substituting the energized experience of Vitality with caffeine, sugar, drugs, sex, arguing, worrying, and such.
Using your environment to induce adrenaline or other illusions of vitality. (Perhaps through TV, movies, books, conversations that promote fear, suspicion or overwhelm.)
Feeling envious, jealous or covetous.
Blaming, complaining or raging.
Gossiping.
Nagging feelings of restlessness.
Refusing or rejecting intimacy with yourself or others.
Feeling numb physically, emotionally, mentally, relationally or spiritually.
Confusing perfection with excellence. (You may strive for excellence. You were born perfect.)
Comparing yourself or others in an attempt to gain rank, demean or compartmentalize.
Inciting arguments — or keeping them going.
Telling lies.
Keeping secrets.
Being reactive or defensive.
Filling your time with busy-work.
Working to exhaustion.
Being over or under your body's healthy weight.
Thinking that if someone wins someone else loses.
Resisting the flow of your emotions.
Believing that sex is your reward or can be used as a punishment.

Neglecting your self-care.
Not feeling "at home" in your own skin.
Being controlling or unsupportable.
Avoiding your sacred practices.
Refusing to nourish or nurture yourself or others.
Looking for validation from others.
Seeking approval.

Soul-Level Attunements of Vitality

When you have Adverse Experiences — or if you want to enhance your Energy Channel of Vitality, here are some simple practices to bring you into a higher state of attunement with Vitality:

Meditate.
Commune with nature. Feel, sense, observe — experience the vitality in your natural surroundings.
Ask yourself, "What am I hungry for?" Listen quietly to hear the answers under the surface.
Journal-dialogue with your body, discover its wisdom for accessing and sustaining Vitality.
Watch films that inspire you to see yourself and all of life with wonder and delight.
Practice gratitude and appreciation.
Intentionally talk about what you love and what you value, infusing your conversations and your self-talk with the energy of your words.
Begin an embodied energy practice that engages you fully, body, mind and soul. (Perhaps African dance or a martial art or Kundalini yoga.)
Give yourself space to express and feel your emotions. (Perhaps listen to music that moves you, emotionally. Allow the music to hold you while you cry, shout, writhe, laugh, rock, or otherwise give physical expression to your emotion.)

Begin a "vitality" journal. Record your thoughts, feelings, sensations, fantasies or memories that bring you into a state of feeling *vital*. Focus on expanding your body-awareness and your internal interpretations of the stimuli.

Surround yourself with people and create environments that enrich your sense of Vitality.

You may also look at the Life-Integration Practices in for any of the Sacred Truths for other practices and ways to enhance your experience of Vitality.

The Energy Channel of Soul Desire

Soul Desire as Embodied Expression

There is a resonance, a vibration that radiates out from your heart as energy waves into the space around you and beyond. Soul Desire transcends time and space and matter, moving out from the spark of light that ignites in you until it finds its resonance-match in the Universe. The image I have is of concentric spherical rings that begin somewhere deep within my being, reaching, expanding out into space. I also see that a series of connections begin to find their way back to me, leading that which I desire to my awareness. It's a beautiful, kinetic network of Desire! I may never know the series of moments that took place and I delight in that.

Perspective of Soul Desire

Remember, perspective is a state of being. Read aloud the following statements and notice the energy of them in your being. These are not affirmations, rather expressions of the *state of being* you may experience when your Energy Channel of Soul Desire is clear and activated.

> Soul Desire resonates in my soul, and from the soul of the universe, guiding me to live a joyous life.
> Soul Desire is my innate navigator for living a joyous, meaningful, purposeful life.
> I joyously attune to my Desire.
> I accept and appreciate the resonance of my Desire as Divine expressing through me.
> I celebrate each and every reflection of Desire as it is revealed to me.
> I courageously and willingly say, "Yes!" to Desire.
> Desire continues to show me the next opportunity for living a joyous, meaningful, generous life. My job is to notice and respond.
> I celebrate the inner and outer vibrations of my Desire.
> I appreciate the beauty of Desire, even when I sometimes don't understand it.
> I partner with my Desire and that of the Universe.
> I honor the power of my mind and focus my thoughts for my highest good.
> I forgive myself any ways in which I have negated my Desire in the past.
> Desire emanates from my heart and soul, sounding a vibrational tone that attunes with the Universe's Desire.
> I listen with softened senses and awareness to the many ways in which my Desire is expressed (Perhaps through dreams, sensation, intuition, ideas, inspiration, in song, tangential thought, in nature, or in dance.)
> Soul Desire is My Unique Key to Living a Life of Joy, Meaning and Love.

I have an intense sense of WellBeing when I experience Soul Desire.

Adverse Experiences of Soul Desire
Signs that you are not experiencing the Energy Channel of Soul Desire as not clear and connected include:

Creating persistent distractions in your life.
Choosing friends who don't pursue their dreams or honor their Desire.
Feeling envious, jealous or covetous.
Blaming, complaining or raging about how you don't live the life you really want to live.
Nagging feelings of restlessness.
Thinking, saying or feeling that you're not worthy of being, doing, having or experiencing your desires.
Feeling ambivalent.
Defending your weaknesses or incompetence.
Saying, "But who am I ... ?"
Saying, "But I'm afraid of being too smart... " (too bright, strong, independent, successful or standing out or being singled out.)
Saying, "But I don't know what I want."
In any way believing that what you want doesn't matter — or that you can't have it.
Working to absolute exhaustion.
Thinking that if someone wins someone else loses.
Believing you can't have what you want.
In any way thinking that what you want is unimportant.
Being unwilling to receive. (Perhaps in the form of inspiration, assistance, payment, gifts or compliments)
Being controlling or unsupportable.
Trying, trying, trying, but not doing the one thing you know needs doing.
Avoiding your sacred practices.
Refusing to celebrate your successes or those of others.

Soul-Level Attunements of Soul Desire

When you have Adverse Experiences — or if you want to enhance your Energy Channel of Soul Desire, here are some simple practices to bring you into a higher state of attunement Soul Desire:

Practice intense gratitude. Not just using words take yourself into the full-on experience of feeling grateful for the many blessings in your life.

Be absolutely clear about what you do know you want.

Say, "Yes!" to opportunities that align with your Soul Desire. (You may want to use the Discernment Process that you'll find later in this section as well.)

Say, "No." when that's the honest, clear answer. Then move on.

Make a commitment — the kind that has no back doors or escape routes — to your Soul Desire.

Ask yourself daily, "How did I close my heart to my Desire today?" Forgive yourself. Then take one action that opens your heart and creates permission for you to experience your Soul Desire as Reality.

Journal-dialogue with your Soul Desire. Write to feel, see, know, touch, taste and imagine ... Bring the energy of your Desire into your full awareness. Make it real, here and now.

Ask for support. Ask in prayer. Ask by journaling. Ask for the ability or connections or willingness that you need.

You may also look at the Life-Integration Practices for any of the Sacred Truths you intuit would support you in developing your Energy Channel of Soul Desire.

Energy shifts in your consciousness and physicality and ripples out into Life. Change does not have to take great lengths of time, nor does it require great effort. Co-creation happens when you are Living in accord with Sacred Truths and fostering your connection with Spirit, Vitality and Desire. That downward spiral into the muck of mediocrity is not your destiny! In every moment, in THIS moment, you can choose to live your Truth. Right now, not next week or next year, or after you meet some criteria. Now.

Free flowing channels of Divinity plus Vitality plus Soul Desire equal living an abundant joyous, meaningful life you love, and being vitally awake in your life.

Joyous Prosperity

You are not here merely to make a living. You are here in order to enable the world to live more amply, with greater vision, with a finer spirit of hope and achievement. You are here to enrich the world, and you impoverish yourself if you forget the errand.

— Woodrow Wilson

The best way to pay for a lovely moment is to enjoy it.

— Richard Bach

Prosperity. Abundance. Wealth. Rich.

These are words I often use to express a meaningful, joyous, purposeful life. Yet there is still a stigma for many of us around the idea of being wealthy, whether financially or in other material forms. Too many spiritual seekers keep themselves from living a thoroughly joyous and expressive life because they are caught up in a tangle of veils around money. Money, in spiritual circles, is often the "don't go there" topic.

You are exquisitely suited to be prosperous, but not because money will bring you joy. Joy is a state of being, not a result of your circumstances. You are exquisitely suited to be prosperous because you are a radiant, expressive soul. You have gifts to bring to light and to share with the world. Your wealth makes it possible for you to experience abundance in the world around you, and to exchange it for experiences that support your growth. Money gives you freedom and with freedom, more choices.

Money — and the talk of it — is everywhere. How many times a day do you hear, say or think about:

> How to make money, save money and spend less.
> Refinancing your mortgage, increasing your pay or taking a cut.
> I can't afford it.
> Commissions earned.
> Pay your bills.
> Credit cards.
> Interest rates.
> Tax increases or are they cuts?
> How much?
> That's too expensive!
> It was on sale!
> It's not in the budget.
> The cost of living.

The cost of health care.
Bankruptcies, foreclosures, and bail-outs.
Lottery winners.
Mismanaged funds.
Windfalls.

Wisdom Key

Joyous Prosperity is an experience of being wealthy in all expressions of your life.

Messages are jumbled up in our heads, online, on TV, in the paper and in nearly every conversation. With all this attention and focus on money, you'd think we would feel wealthy, be aware of our abundance and prosperity, but most of us don't.

You are prosperous, wealthy and abundant. Sacred Truths show us that we are each part of the whole, and whole unto ourselves. When you shift your understanding of prosperity to a whole-life expression of good fortune, you'll see that prosperity is a state of WellBeing. As you integrate Sacred Truths you can choose to create wealth and prosperity in any and every area of your life — inner and outer, material and spiritual, relational and individual.

Earlier I mentioned the collective shift in consciousness that is changing our world. In part, this Global Shift invites us to see ourselves, and the world, with new perspectives of unity and wholeness — rather than the dualities we have been focusing on. Dualities show us that we are not honoring Soul. Soul always introduces a third perspective or possibility.

One of the ways this illusion of duality was set in place happened hundreds of years ago when powers-that-be made agreements that spirit and science would be governed by two separate power-bodies, and they would not acknowledge or permit intermingling of the two.

Those power-bodies were mimicking early stages of human development when we perceive ourselves as separate, compartmentalized: ethereal or material, but not both. Ah, but that is not Truth. You are whole, not divided nor segmented. Yet, our ancestors collectively and unconsciously internalized this cultural lie. Then so did we.

Wisdom Key

You are whole, complete.

Today, the veils we wear perpetuate a divide between inner and outer, spirit and science, intuition and proof, poverty and prosperity. I'm sure you've known people who are financially wealthy, yet perpetually unhappy in their relationships — or they are spiritually bereft. Others are spiritually rich, but never have any money or struggle to be productive. Some are physically wealthy (healthy), yet they are emotionally bankrupt. Do you recognize yourself in a variation of these dualities, conflicts between inner and outer, various expressions of prosperity?

Sacred Truths show us that you are *infinite* which means you have access to infinite resources. Joyous Prosperity is an experience of being wealthy in all expressions of your life that matter to you.

Creating a life you love always includes both:

a healthy, prosperous inner life, a*nd*
a rich, rewarding, purposeful outer life.

Many of the cultural veils we don suggest that money is not spiritual. That perhaps you should not even dare to want it, that frugality — even poverty — is more righteous than wealth. Such ideas are veils, not Truth. In his book, *The Science of Getting Rich,* Wallace Wattles takes a compelling and fervent stand for wealth — financial, monetary wealth — and for joyous prosperity. Reading this powerful little book is like going to a wealth counselor and a spiritual teacher in the same uplifting, transformational session. One statement Wattles wrote that I wish to share with you is this:

> *"You want to get rich in order that you may eat, drink and be merry when it is time to do these things; in order that you may surround yourself with beautiful things, see distant lands, feed your mind, and develop your intellect; in order that you may love men and do kind things, and be able to play a good part in helping the world to find truth."*

This is a quintessential expression of Joyous Prosperity! Wealth makes it possible for you to live your Soul's Divine Purpose more fully — without veiled-restrictions that suggest you are not worthy, incapable or somehow not supposed to experience prosperity, abundance, wealth and riches. Wealth fuels you with greater capacity to serve, celebrate, experience, contribute to all that you appreciate!

How Much Can You Bare?

And forget not that the earth delights to feel your bare feet and the winds long to play with your hair.

— Kahlil Gibran

Alright, so here you are, shedding your veils of illusion. What happens as you bare your true self? Are you left standing there, naked, for all to see?

The impulse to cover up, or return to your comfort-zone of familiarity, can be quite strong. Like a large rubber band snapping back after being stretched out to it's expanded length. S-N-A-P!

As you create a new or expanded reality, a richer, joyous experience, the magnetic pull of history and habit will tug at you, trying to bring you back to the familiar, to your former comfort zone — back to defining yourself with limitations rather than embracing your new reality.

You have a comfort-zone for everything. How much intimacy you can tolerate or how little. How much income, how little. How much joy, how little. The same goes for body weight, luxury, success, recognition, giving and receiving. As your veils fall away, you will feel vulnerable in this new way of being. You will be out of your comfort-zone. You may be tempted to retrieve old veils — even unknowingly, and drape them again over your eyes.

If your goal is to stay comfortable, you will find an unveiled path unsettling. However if you want to love and be loved, be creative, to grow, if you want to live at your highest potential, to express your magnificence in the world, then know this: You are going to continue to experience discomfort.

I witnessed this some years ago with one man I worked with. There was a great divide between how much Ari would allow himself to experience and what he truly wanted. A man of deep thought and intense feelings, he longed to pursue his spiritual studies and decided to attend a two-week retreat in the high desert. He signed up, raised the funds to attend and pay for his travel, made all the preparations to be away for that length of time, and when it was just about time to go, he called me to drop out. Then six months later, when the next retreat was scheduled, he signed up, paid, was set to go. Again, Ari called to cancel just days before the retreat began.

Each time he retracted was painful for him — and for me. Each time he denied himself what he truly desired, he recoiled in shame and disappointment. As his spiritual guidance counselor at the time, I felt compassion for his desire and for the pain of refusing it. I remembered my own experiences of denying Desire. If you've ever felt a deep desire for something that you experienced as a call from your Soul — and refused to allow yourself to have it, you know the kind of torment he was creating for himself.

His desire was great. As is often true with spiritual initiations or the practice of meditation, we don't know what we will experience or develop, simply that we are called. While Ari battled with his inner dialog of "Go. Don't Go," he shared his intention with his older brother, the patriarch of the family, a man he respected and appreciated.

His brother's adamant stance was: "Don't go! Stay here. Work your business. Get yourself established in the real world."

Ari's perceptions of himself that said he couldn't have what he truly wanted rang out, agreeing with his brother. Ambivalence is often an indication of some unconscious commitments that keep you stuck, preventing you from experiencing the discomfort of growing, expanding, living fully — while at the same time perpetuating a sense of uneasiness and upset that won't resolve. Ari was caught in this ambivalence. He had not made the commitment to his Desire. That commitment would have helped him transcend the push-me-pull-you game he was in. Neither had he made the decision to walk away, putting it all to rest, for good.

The third time he signed up, he went. When he did, he stepped into a new way of being. His perception of himself grew as did his deeper, more grounded spirituality. A year later he went again! He expanded his comfort-zone until he could sustain the level of being.

Ari has matured as a man and as a spiritual being. He is courageous with his desire, and has learned to translate the experience he had all those years ago, applying it to other areas of his life. For instance, the man he was even 5 years ago was not able to create an intimate relationship. Yet, just a few months ago I attended his wedding to a beautiful, loving woman. I suspect we'll see them beginning a family soon.

Stepping into your own Joyous, Prosperous, Radiant Self will be at times challenging, even painful — and some of the people in your life may speak loudly against it, as Ari's brother did.

Anais Nin wrote, "And the day came when the risk to remain tight in a bud was more painful than the risk it took to blossom." Comfort in the old familiar places can become claustrophobic and imprisoning, just as the tight bud does. While the unknown may feel like a great risk, your blossoming potential is there, ready for you to open.

Raise Your Comfort

Whatever your level of comfort, you have grown accustomed to keeping yourself in that zone. We each tend to have a range: only so low, only so high, no more, no less. Even if you are unhappy with that range, it feels better to be in it than to be pushing past the limits — in either direction. This range tends to feel safe, familiar, habitual and often boring. You might not be tight in the bud, but you are also not blossoming. This kind of comfort is a slow killer to your passion and joy. It's the place that slowly suffocates your dreams and what they're made of. This is the place that "A-ha moments" are made for — attempting to wake us up and pop us out of the illusion that says, "comfort is good."

Dreams can never be realized in this zone. But how do you know where you are in it? And then, how do you break out? You begin with awareness.

Sacred Truths

Just as with any meditation practice, the best place to start is where you are. Here is an exercise that will help you assess and expand your awareness. It will give you a glimpse at your current comfort "temperature." As you make even the slightest shifts in your energy and awareness — which is exactly what happens as you integrate Sacred Truths — you can change your temperatures... often by great leaps, sometimes incrementally. The assessment will give you perspective on where you are may be resisting your essential, radiant Self.

You'll need a pencil. Set it by your side.

> Close your eyes.
> Receive three slow, easy breaths — fully inhale, fully exhale.
> Let your attention drop into your body, into your inner wisdom.
> Now, simply take your "temperature" in each of the following areas.
>
> On a thermometer of 0 — 100,
> 0 is stone-cold broke;
> 100 is abundant, joyous, soulful, delicious wealth.
>
> How prosperous, how fully connected, expressive and joyous do you feel at this time?
>
> > Spiritual
> > Purpose & Meaning

Physical
Intimacy
Sexuality
Relationships
Finance
Livelihood — Your Work/Career
Community
Home
Environment
Frame of Mind
Emotional WellBeing
Education / Learning
Integrity — Being True to Yourself
Security
Self-Appreciation
Love
Joy, Bliss, Rapture

____

____

(Add areas of importance to you.)

Your temperature ratings will give you a sense of where you allow and choose fullness, joy and wealth in your life, and where you are resisting it.

This exercise is not meant to bring you shame or upset. Low temperatures simply show you the veils that keep you feeling stuck, alone or frustrated.

If I had done this exercise in late 1999, my spiritual temperature would have been upwards of 100, while my livelihood and finance would have been 37 and 54, respectively. My work was meaningful — I was being of service to thousands of people — but the exhausting hours I kept and the low pay I got in return were anything but prosperous. I was depleted and feeling broke.

At the time there was a media blitz about what might happen when the clocks in computers rolled over to 2000. There were fears that power grids, communications and finance systems could all go haywire, and roll across the globe as the new millennium issued in. My intuition told me all would be fine. Yet I had a private fantasy that Y2K would cause at least some of the problems forecast so I wouldn't have to go back to work after January 1st. While I felt ashamed to be hoping for a global meltdown, I also saw it as a wake-up call. When fantasies, ideas or your dreams suggest that something you want is not for the betterment of all, there is always a veil disguising your Soul Desire.

My momentary fantasy showed me, as I used it to gaze inward, that I was wishing someone would press a reset button — that all the power grids, communications and finances would start anew. I thought of when a computer seizes and the only solution left is to reboot. I didn't want a global reset; I wanted it for myself, a reboot on *my* power, communications and finances.

On New Year's Eve 1999 I watched the celebrations of the dawning of the year 2000 on TV, starting in the farthest reaches of the earth, rolling around the planet's time zones, one country or continent after another with music, fireworks, dancing, prayer. The celebrations contrasted with my weariness.

I decided it was time to change what I was creating in my own corner of the world. This was not a New Year's resolution. It was a choice to co-create a new experience in my life.

I mentioned earlier that if you choose to answer the call to your magnificence, you must open your heart and mind, and take mature responsibility for your choices. I chose to do just that. I began removing veils that no longer served me. Whatever kept me from living my Soul's Divine Purpose and fulfilling my own dreams, I began to let it go.

Shifting my energy and awareness created huge changes — immediately. I didn't work harder or longer to do it. My livelihood and finances aligned with my highest good, as I shifted my *being*. I started teaching new programs and leading retreats. The owners of the company I worked with invited me to co-lead all of their new programs, nationwide. I was reaching and serving more people — and felt well used as a teacher and spiritual counselor. My "reboot" expanded to my physical sense of vitality, the more energy work I led and taught, the more essential it was that my body be well loved, nourished and fit. I took up a martial art called Kendo. I incorporated Bikram yoga and spin classes into my spiritual practices. I lost weight. Over the next two years my relationships grew more intimate and my creativity soared. And I met my beloved, sweetheart Michael.

The Power of Discernment

As far as we can discern, the sole purpose of existence is to kindle a light in the darkness of mere being.

— Carl Jung

Discernment is a powerful tool of personal freedom. The Latin origin of the word *discern, discernere,* means: *dis-* "off, away" and *cernere* "distinguish, separate, sift." Discernment separates away whatever was clouding your view of yourself, of your life and your potential. As you integrate Sacred Truths, you sift through what fits with Truth and that which does not that can be separated-away.

Often I hear from mentoring clients that confusion or overwhelm is so upsetting and off-putting that they want to make it go away. "Stop the confusion! End the Overwhelm!" In their reaction to make it stop, they latch onto anything that relieves their discomfort. Or they find someone to blame for their circumstances. Or they justify not wanting what they want, saying, "It's too big or too much or too hard... or too scary." They are unwilling to sacrifice the familiar for their higher good. Do this repeatedly, over years, and life feels void of passion, creativity or purpose.

When you feel confused or overwhelmed, consider this: You have received an invitation to stop doing or thinking that which is not aligned with your Soul's Divine Purpose. It's as if a light is being shown on a veil that is ready for your attention and removal. As you discern — separate away — that which does not serve your highest good, your Purpose or your Soul Desire, concerns that once seemed looming and ominous lose their zest and influence over you.

I share with you the Discernment Process, a simple 3 part series of steps you can use to make decisions, or for soul-level discovery. First, let's look at the four energetic qualities that aid that process: Courage, Curiosity, Compassion and Clarity.

Courage: Open your heart, brave one.

When we watched Dorothy and her friends follow the yellow brick road to Oz, we heard the Cowardly Lion bemoan, "If I only had the nerve." The Wizard's answer to him was a ribbon of courage. Courage is of the heart. It is the quality that aligns heart with action.

A participant in a workshop I was leading wanted to share his Soul's Purpose with the group. He sat without speaking for what must have seemed like an eternity to him, then turned to me and said, "I want to do this, but I'm afraid." I reminded him — and all of us in the room — that courage is what we call on in the face of fear, not the absence of it.

I guided him to access courage in his heart. He closed his eyes, placed his hand at his heart, truly felt his connection to his Purpose, and his desire to share it. Then as he opened his eyes and looked out at the men and women in the circle — with a tremble in his voice — he said it. Then he said it again.

The third time he moved his body in his seat, took a full breath, and spoke clearly the embodied expression of his message. We all witnessed a moment of courage.

Often we think we want to be courageous, and imagine that means we won't feel nervous, tummy-fluttering, voice-quivering anxiousness. In our goal-driven culture and with years of touting, "feel the fear and do it anyway," we forgot the essential meaning of courage: of the heart.

In the face of your physical, emotional and mental fear responses, you can choose to open your heart and connect to your Soul Desire. That's what is on the other side of the fear. Step courageously into your Self and a new experience of living. Transcending your comfort-zone requires courage. Having an "audacity to believe" begs you to step into courage — so that you may enact the change you believe in.

There is physical, body-felt experience of courage for each of us. The man in the workshop felt it in the center of his chest, activated by the touch of his hand to his Heart Chakra. By the simple act of touching a place on your body or moving a certain way, you can ignite and activate the energy of courage in you. Notice if there is a place in, on or around your body that guides you to experience courage.

Curiosity: Open your mind.

Curiosity is to the mind what courage is to the heart. A curious mind — as it aids in discernment — seeks to reveal Truth and opportunity, and promote WellBeing. Activate curiosity with your imagination, with playful pondering. Anticipate that there may be more than meets your eye at first glance.

As with courage there is a physical, body-felt experience — or gesture — of curiosity, often associated with a hand on the face or the head, or gazing outwardly. I picture Albert Einstein perhaps sitting, toking on a cigar; or gazing into a starry sky. By the simple act of touching a place on your body or moving a certain way you can ignite and activate the energy of curiosity in you. Notice if there is a place in, on or around your body that opens you to a state of curiosity.

You can enhance your open-minded curiosity even further when you begin a question with the words, "I wonder..." I learned this technique from Gay Hendricks who discovered that by adding these words, and a little hum, like: "Hmmm.... I wonder...," a person becomes even more playful in his pondering, opening to a greater sense of curiosity.

Curious Questions to Incite Wonder: Here are examples of questions that are fundamentally curious. You may want to say a few of these out loud as you read them, beginning with "Hmm... I wonder..." and a gesture or touch that enhances your curiosity. Light-heartedness will bring more to mind. Try it a few times now for yourself.

- I wonder... Where is the joy and ease in this moment?
- I wonder... If I knew my next step, what might it be?
- I wonder... How may I be of service?

- I wonder... What might create more intimacy in my relationship?
- I wonder... How could I express my purpose (desire, talent, intention) at this time?
- I wonder... Why am I so darn happy? or healthy, loved, generous, beautiful? (I love how a question like this one presupposes an outcome that may not yet exist in your awareness!)

When you are feeling stuck, these are the types of questions that can shift your energy and thought with wonder and curiosity.

- I wonder... How does this thought (belief, rule, expectation, action) serve?
- I wonder... What I could change in this moment that would shift my experience?
- I wonder... How might this work?
- I wonder... What is a third possibility? (helps get out of the either-or frame of mind)
- I wonder... Who could help with this...even if I don't yet know them?
- I wonder... If I were seeing the Truth in this, what might it be?
- I wonder... If there were an easy, graceful, creative solution to this, what might it be?
- I wonder... What I am unconsciously resisting?
- I wonder... What do I need to do (let go of, ask for) to have the experience I desire?

These are just a few ideas to get you in a curiosity frame of mind. I suggest you make a list of questions you can ask yourself and others when you want to open your mind to possibility and opportunity. Ponder any given question for a period of time, days or even weeks.

Uncurious — Just So You Know: Let's take a look at questions that do not promote curiosity (and are commonly asked.)

- Why me?
- What's wrong with me (them, this)?
- Why I am always _____? (filled in with some kind of victim word like the scapegoat, left out, singled out, falling behind, picking up the slack, alone, ahead of everyone else).
- What's so great about them? Why do they get ____ (fill in your blank) and I don't?
- I am smart (have done it before, have money, should be able to do this). Why can't I figure this out?
- Why do I keep making the same mistake over and over again?
- How am I supposed to ____ (fill in with what you want) when ___ (fill in with what you think limits you)? (As in: How am I supposed to <u>start a new business</u> when <u>we're in a nationwide financial crises</u>? Or: How can <u>I tell the truth about what I really want</u> when <u>I have so many obligations to fill already</u>.)

As you can see, un-curious questions tend to be blaming, victim-minded, justifying that a problem is bigger than you or they perpetuate duality-thinking, or they presuppose that there is no elegant, soulful solution.

Embodied Imagination: Another way you can access curiosity is to consider how someone else might respond. I once had a dream that featured Robert Redford in a meeting with some investors. I learned so much from him through the exploration of my dream that I have sometimes asked myself, "How would Robert Redford see this situation?" I have no idea what the man would do, but my inner Robert Redford is a clear-headed, compassionate visionary who guides me to consider my ponderings differently. You may do this with an imagined or real person. Perhaps you'll ask, "What would Buddha do, or Jesus?" Your source may be a mythical goddess, an elder, an ancestor, a great scientist, a young child, or even elemental — perhaps the sun, or a tree, or an image from a dream.

Compassion: A loving experience of understanding.

Compassion is a state of being, not something you do. Compassion brings deep understanding and releases any sense of shame or blame of anything you may have done or not done, said or not said, felt or not felt.

We're looking at compassion specifically as it relates to discernment. It is much broader and more powerful than this. However, it is such an important part of the discernment process that I primarily refer to it as it applies to being compassionate with yourself.

As you are compassionate with yourself, you cease to hold yourself captive by the past. You release yourself from shackles that kept you small, afraid, angry or in any way a victim.

Compassion for yourself and others is a way of being. Reach for it from within. Curiously, ask yourself, "I wonder...

how do I feel compassion in my body?" Notice if there is a place in, on or around your body that brings you into a state compassion.

When you enter the Discernment Process you may become aware of judgments you have. Breathing and allowing yourself to feel what lies beneath the judgment will create space for you to continue and to sift, sort and separate away.

Clarity: Truth will set you free!

With clarity you see what is important. You see the big picture and how the smaller parts fit in. Anything that is unnecessary warrants just a moment of time or energy. When you feel a pebble in your shoe, you stop for a moment, take off your shoe, remove the problem, assess any damage done, and attend to it as needed. Before you know it you're walking along as if it never happened.

The same is true when you have clarity. With it you no longer spend your energy or time in confusion, cynicism, doubt, shame, blame ... and other such thoughts and feelings. You notice them like the pebble in your shoe. Stop a moment. Look to see if there's a cause or damage that requires attention. When you have clarity, you don't get lost following the crumbs, or bright, shiny distractions. You may periodically pause to see if there is a way you are being that creates an attractive environment for distractions or obstacles.

While pure will and personal drive rarely bring you into clarity, Sacred Truths always do. As you integrate them with conscious commitment into your life, clarity, along with courage, curiosity and compassion, grows within you.

You may have embodied experiences of clarity. Ask yourself, "How does clarity feel in my body?" Notice if there is a place in, on or around your body that feels to you like clarity.

The Discernment Process

You can use the Discernment Process to discern (separate away) something that is troubling you, as in the case of feeling overwhelmed or frustrated or disappointed. Use this if you are feeling ambivalent about a decision you are facing — or if you are presented with an opportunity that you aren't sure about. As you practice it, you may find that it becomes second nature, a simple series of steps you walk yourself through to clarity and choice.

Step 1 - Aware Assessment

Breathe.
Bring your awareness to the present.
Attune your energy and focus to your Soul Desire.
Notice what is stirred up or what you are experiencing that poses a question for you.
Notice the thought, emotion, sensation, idea or opportunity that is in your attention.

State or clarify the opportunity, thought, emotion, sensation or idea that you are considering.

During Step 1 you may be called on to tap into courage, or to stir things up with curiosity. You may find that compassion is required of you as you face the question at hand. If you take this step on, you will find clarity in the question you are considering.

Step 2 - Focused Inquiry

This is where courage and curiosity come into the process. Have the courage to face not just the questions, but **also** your answers, your Truth. Be curious, following the underlying feelings, sensations, ideas that come up as you go through each of the focusing questions.

While each of these questions can all be answered with "Yes-No," you may also notice that your response includes "And." When that happens, the "and" is an indication to start again with Aware Assessment.

1. Do I want this? Do I want what it promotes, what it stands for?
2. Does this align with my Soul's Divine Purpose?
3. Does this align with my Soul Desire?
4. Is this in accord with Sacred Truths, promoting the highest good for all?
5. Does this do harm to or violate the rights of others or myself?

Step 3 - Choice Point

Decision Choice Point: If you are using the Discernment Process for considering an opportunity, the results of your Focused Inquiry reveal your answer. If you answer yes to 1, 2, 3, 4, and no to 5, then your choice is clear to say yes to the opportunity. When you have any other combination of responses, you have discerned that your choice is to decline.

Soulful Choice Point: If you are, instead, discerning a thought, emotion, sensation or such, each step in the process leads you to uncover or dissolve a veil. You can deepen your inquiry as well, taking your exploration to a soul level. When you answer each question above, also notice how do you feel, what do you sense or experience in your body, what images emerge? Use a drawing journal or a dance floor or a park or a hot tub for soulful discovery and discernment.

I have used and honed this process over many years and now teach it to my private clients. It is a powerful and useful tool that I invite you to begin using now and to return to over and over again. As you do, be compassionate with yourself. Removing veils of illusion may bring up emotions, sensations, memories and ideas that feel really uncomfortable and upsetting. That's to be expected — you are very familiar with the illusions. You've learned to navigate your life by looking through them.

While I have used the Discernment Process for a very long time, I discovered a new, expanded perspective in it when I met David Neagle, who teaches a similar process. I learned from David that none of the questions in Step 2 leave room for qualifiers like "If I could afford it," "When I prove myself worthy," "But only if my friend, partner, family, spouse, children agree." Those qualifiers do not play a part in discerning. Instead, they are separated away, leaving you with a clear decision. Your decision ends the query. Either it is, "Yes," you decide that you are choosing this, or "No," you are not. Simple.

Breaking Free

Humankind is being led along an evolving course,
through this migration of intelligences,
and though we seem to be sleeping,
there is an inner wakefulness
that directs the dream,
and that will eventually startle us back
to the truth of who we are.

— Jalal ad-Din Rumi

I have a personal story to share with you. One I offer with the highest intention to show you that transformation is possible and sustainable — and that Sacred Truths and the processes I present in this book provide a map to living an abundant, joyous and meaningful life.

Today I am one of the most joyous people I know. I am filled with wonder and appreciation — and an intention to bring my gifts to the world, generously and in grace. I have a passion for life that emanates from within, compelling me to live fully. I partner with other high-vision, high-purpose leaders in ways that continue to delight and grow me, personally, professionally and spiritually. This is much of the life I quietly, privately dreamed of when I was growing up, and as a young woman. I sensed my soul was calling me, guiding me to live a life that was true to me — that I was filled with potential and it was my job to live into it. I remember standing at the kitchen window, when I was perhaps 10, seeing a glimpse forward in time: me, a woman, traveling the world, independent and wise.

Soulful moments such as these were my lifeline, leading me along the path that would deliver me from a self-imposed illusion — a most insidious veil. You see, even as I touched moments of grace and soulful connection, my predominant experience was of being essentially unlovable. I didn't have this language for it, but this veil tainted most of my world, most of the time. With it came a coating over my heart, my mind, my perceptions of myself and the world around me.

There was evidence, if you looked at the circumstances of my life that would tell you clearly that I was loved. I cannot say that my parents did anything to promote my pain and struggle. I had friends, family, lovers, even a husband, who I suspect, on most levels, never knew that my experience of myself was as an unlovable. Yet at a very early age — perhaps before I was even born — I donned this inner veil and lived with its deep, private pain.

This is the kind of veil that eludes detection, often for a lifetime. When you can't see it, when it's so mixed in with the fibers of your being, you don't know that you are living inside a lie. I had no idea, except that I felt misunderstood, unworthy, and a persistent sense of dissatisfaction. I thought I just had ambition, a drive to create something in the world, something meaningful. I thought my ambition is what gave me a consistent sense of unrest. My unconscious motivation was to find or do something that would prove me worthy of Love. Ambition got channeled in two directions, the first out of reaction to my underlying view of myself and the world; the other in response to it, which led me to discover Sacred Truths.

Reacting Gives an Illusion Power

My reaction — to the illusion (belief or veil) that I was unlovable — was to perform and produce. At a young age I focused all that drive into school, scouts, churches, theater and choir. By the time I was twenty I started my first real business, and soon became a leader in my community. I was well known and respected for the quality of my services, products and staff. I invested in myself as a business owner by hiring a consulting firm that Michael Gerber founded.

My coach (that's the term we would use today) was fascinated by my business and systems, but somehow we never got around to the essential component of pricing and profitability. That business never made any money. My underlying belief told me "if I didn't give-away-the-store, I wouldn't have any clients." When I just couldn't do it any more I sold the name of the company and all the supplies and equipment to someone who never paid me for them. Then I never pursued her. I thought if I were worthy of being paid what she owed me, I wouldn't have to ask.

I tell you this early business experience to demonstrate a point: the veils we don alter our thinking, our emotions and reasoning. As a businesswoman I would tell you, of course I needed to charge fees that would result in profits. But I didn't. I would say that when you hire a coach to support you in your business, it's your responsibility to get the support from him or her that will lead to more profit, better service and quality of life that you desire. And when you have a sales agreement, verbal or written, if you don't take a stand in asking for what you want, you are doing a disservice to yourself, your family and the person with whom you made the agreement.

I can say all that, but from inside the illusion-veil that I lived under, I couldn't see, act or ask for what I wanted. Being unlovable — for me — meant being unworthy of all forms of appreciation, including money. Every business endeavor that followed, for the next 20 years, was a repeat of that same story — different companies, people, circumstances, cities and degrees of loss, but the same story, the same me.

But I wasn't a constant failure. There was an upside to every business I owned, or company I worked for, including the people I met and worked with, the lives I touched with my innate gifts of warmth and understanding and my creativity. I was the top producing sales-designer for several companies and managing director of a national training company. I became a featured speaker, a workshop leader and a published writer. I produced at least a thousand events, weddings, seminars and retreats. I have been a spiritual guidance counselor, coach and mentor who brings a deep compassion and conviction that my clients live into their potential and Purpose; all of this seemed to be in spite of the illusion-veil I wore.

Still, no achievements ever relieved my struggle or soothed my pain. They never could. They never will. When you live under a veil as pervasive and evasive as mine was — and I believe we all have them — you are always in the illusion it creates. That illusion colors everything with its tainted perspective. So, for me, if I achieved, I was still unlovable. When I failed at any relationship, business or dream, I knew inside that it was because I was unlovable. No matter how hard you try, you cannot break free from an illusion by changing something "out there." But try, I did!

I felt alone. I was angry that I couldn't break free of the persistent sorrow in my heart. I longed for intimacy and connection, silently crying myself to sleep many nights, even when I was married, as my husband lay in bed next to me. Mine was a private pain. How could I allow anyone to see me, lost and lonely? I believed I must keep my shameful experience a secret. (Secrets — a dangerous form of veils — keep us from ever living in the full light and expression of our radiance.)

I was confused by incongruence. How could I be smart, creative, courageous and talented, have friends who respected, trusted and admired me, and feel as lost to my true self as I did?

Responding to an Awakening Soul

While in the midst of all that angst and effort, a still, quiet calling drew me toward the path that would lead me to Love, to Meaning, and to Joy.

The first meditation class I attended was a long time ago. I was, I think, 14. I was by far the youngest person in an old church in Oakland, California where a few hundred people gathered as Betty Bethards led us in meditation and energy work. My mother brought me with her — I'm not sure why. Many opportunities happened like that, through synchronicity or intuition: I would discover a book, attend a class, listen to a cassette tape or receive an invitation that would lead me to the next signpost on the path of my soul. I dedicated years of my life to studying the mystic arts, energy systems and flow, mythology, human consciousness and world religions. I found that I was adept in the language of the Soul, and guided hundreds, perhaps thousands of people in experiencing it for themselves.

Wisdom Key

You are whole, perfect, beautiful, just as you are. Embrace your highest nature.

I was always compelled to learn, grow and develop, hoping that I would one day wake up with a sense of freedom and WellBeing. I discovered the most fundamental Truth: I was not broken. I was not unlovable. I was and am whole, radiant, exquisite, as are we all! As are you! I transformed as I unveiled my radiance, removing layers of that audacious lie until it no longer imprisoned me, until I was free. Freedom is as available to us as bondage: two sides of the same coin. Sacred Truths show you how to flip it to the side of Freedom.

I learned to soften my senses until I could hear the resonance of Soul Desire — and saw that it had been there all along, showing me the way, if only I could see, feel, hear and accept it. The inkling I had at a young age that my life was meant to have meaning — each of our lives is — finally became clear as I reached my hand out in acceptance of my Soul's Divine Purpose. Along the path, I discovered my capacity to Believe. I courageously and persistently learned to Act in Faith, and to Trust myself and Life.

You are whole, perfect, beautiful, just as you are. And from an unveiled moment along your path, you can grow — not out of reaction, but rather in an embrace of your highest nature. Sacred Truths reveal the radiance of your soul, and veils dissolve as you integrate Truths into your life. You don't need to go look for what is broken or eluding detection. The work is to fully immerse yourself in the energy of Truths.

I was able to shine the light of my own soul's radiance bright enough that even I could see the veil that had been my constant companion for nearly 50 years. That veil, if not gone completely, is now thin and more easily detected when lingering fibers reappear like clingy tendrils of a well-rooted vine.

Today, I can tell you: I am a gift of Love.

Try this for moment: say aloud, "I am a gift of Love."

Notice how you feel when you say the words. When I first said them, I could only whisper, chokingly, and hoped no one would hear.

Now again, breathe in, and as you exhale, "I am a gift of Love."

Perhaps you can imagine what a transformation it is for a self-imprisoned, self-identified unlovable person to now stand so firmly as an advocate for Love, and for Truths.

For more than two years I even hosted ***Joy of Love and Life*** radio show dedicated to Love! I invited other spiritual teachers, healers and new thought leaders from around the world to join me in joyous, intimate conversations. They shared experiences of Love. We talk about spirituality, relationships, cooking, travel, philanthropy, life purpose, dreams, quantum science, parenting, healing, the arts, creativity, gratitude... the possibilities are endless! Love expands as we engage with the energy. I bask in the miracle of transformation.

So, I ask you: What lies do you tell about yourself, your life? How are you veiled in perceived limitations? Who do you tell? Are yours lies of omission and secrecy? Or perhaps you lie through ambivalence, which can sound like this: You want something with all your heart, and also entertain thoughts that say, "Nah, it's not that important." There you are, left in the dance between two worlds, unfulfilled.

Your lies may be as entangled into your sense of yourself as mine were, maybe not about being loveable, but some other way in which you are limited or excused from being your greatness. You may try to convince yourself it's not a lie, or it's just a small one, or no one will notice, but that's simply not True. Any lies of any size prevent you from living in joyous prosperity and meaning and Love.

While my journey may have taken many years, the changes I see happening in the world today show me that shifts in consciousness take place with great ease and speed, unlike any time before. I watch my clients break free of illusions and sustain their transformations more readily then I did early on. Perhaps they are aided by me, witness and facilitator, as I contribute to the ease and grace they experience; and by a collective of, I believe, millions of people who are ready today to live joyous, meaningful lives, and to Love. For that I rejoice!

Seeing your illusions for what they are: veils, can be tricky. Remember they don't want to be detected, and you've agreed not to notice them or know about them with unconscious commitments you've made over time.

The breeze at dawn has secrets to tell you.
Don't go back to sleep.
You must ask for what you really want.
Don't go back to sleep.

People are going back and forth across the doorsill
where the two worlds touch.

The door is round and open.
Don't go back to sleep.
— Jalal ad-Din Rumi

Co-Creating Your Life

There are only two ways to live your life. One is as though nothing is a miracle. The other is as though everything is a miracle.

— Albert Einstein

One of my lifetime favorite terms is: *Co-Creation*. I love pondering words, saying them repeatedly to myself, hearing them, feeling the sound and vibrations of the words, allowing their meanings to infuse me. The energy of co-creation gives me a sense that I'm not playing this game by myself. There are so many others involved.

Co-Creation reminds us to partner with Source, and to allow that which is greater than our personal will to contribute, inspire and make way for new experiences and opportunities. It also reminds us that there are other people who can and want to create with us, who have gifts that enhance ours, and to whom we can contribute. Co-Creation invites us to expand our consciousness as two or more are gathered in service to something beyond our individual needs. It inspires collaboration and cooperation, resulting in synergy and otherwise unlikely opportunities.

Co-creation is three-dimensional and interwoven. Here are the essential steps in co-creation:

Vision

Clearly see what you desire. Vibrationally, emotionally attune with it. Release what is not your vision. Be clear not to include limitations that you do not actually want. Engage your Infinite Powerful Self, and your Soul Desire, and Believe in your Vision.

Embodied Imagination

Expand and energize your imagination to fully engage your body in your Vision. See, feel and experience it as real. Vitalize your vision. Release or transform that which does not belong or fit. Engage your Body as the Temple of Your Soul in service to your Vision.

Appreciate

Feel and express appreciation for everything. Consciously and continuously appreciate all that you are, experience, have or do. Pray with praise for all the richness and beauty that is your life. Fall in love with your life. Infuse everything — your thoughts, relationships, environment, work and belongings — with Loving Appreciation.

Request

Ask for what you want — no matter how small or how grand. Ask for ideas, resources, invitations, surprises, whatever will support you in Co-Creation. Pray. From inside your Vision, ask, "What is my next step?" Trust that your requests will be granted — even if not directly or in the way you think they should.

Open

Allow yourself to be contributed to. Be open to guidance, ideas and support. Allow synchronicity, opportunities and inspiration to come to you and from within. Open to your intuition. Open to inspiration — divine and otherwise. Allow others to support you. Listen deeply.

Aligned Action

Align your actions — all of your actions — with your vision/desire. Act in Faith.

Receive

Let life happen and flow. Accept and celebrate what comes!

Each of these steps is required in order to co-create with intention. I have found that you must start with the first two: Vision and Embodiment, beyond that, the steps do not follow numerical order — they are all active all the time. You are in perpetual motion, even in stillness.

Aligned Action

Here, where I live, in the United States, we have a collective value for achievement, growth and action. A value that has both served us well and created a great deal of unrest. We have built a strong nation with a great deal of wealth. Opportunities abound. Yet our souls are calling out for balance, for play and joyful rest, for creative expression for the pure experience of creating — not because of the potential profit or a demanding market.

We long for authenticity and intimacy. We yearn to make a difference, but are so busy with obligations and keeping up all we've built that it often seems that there just isn't time for that. We're in a tug-of-war with ourselves, and with each other. We agreed long ago to a competitive model and use it to determine how one qualifies to earn more, have more and experience more.

The Global Shift we're experiencing now is our collective invitation to shake up the dualities we've been identified with. I wonder if we will move to a model of "cooperation and collaboration," and shift to appreciating the value that each of us brings their gifts and life force to the service of others is honored and valued with as much abundance and accolades as we now shower on entertainers, athletes, business icons and politicians — or stars of reality TV.

As we usher in this Global Shift, we are called to action. Not action that is driven to overcome and out-perform others we've known in the past. The action we are called to now is Aligned Action. You might think of it as a shift from left-brain dominated action to whole-brain inspired action.

Wisdom Key

You are the co-creator of this glorious life of yours. Welcome the support!

You are the Co-creator of this glorious life of yours. Design your own map, paved with Sacred Truths. To live the life we've been exploring here you must take consistent action, Aligned Action. I'm not talking about busy for the sake of busy-ness, or duty alone. Aligned Action asks you to consider your choices from one moment to the next, day after day.

Aligned Action puts you in motion:

> Led by your Infinite Self and Soul's Divine Purpose,
> Navigated by your Soul Desire,
> Infused with Love,
> Being honest with yourSelf,
> In perpetual Belief, Faith and Trust, and
> Honoring your Body and Soul.

Ask yourself, "What am I inspired to do at this time, that fulfills my Soul's Divine Purpose, and moves me even more fully into my Desire?" You won't always feel inspired. Sometimes you'll know what the step before you is, and you will resist it. You won't want to make a call, or apologize for something, or make a commitment, or say, "No" to a friend. You may be afraid to do what is unfamiliar or feels vulnerable to you. Or you'll watch TV or indulge in gossip or complaining when you know those actions are not aligned with your glorious, radiant soul. In those moments it helps to have a journal, a trusted friend or mentor — or a book like this one — to remind you to return to your connection (to Divinity, Vitality or Soul Desire.)

Wisdom Key
Be receptive and creative in your actions.

Aligned Action includes supreme self-care, which sometimes leads to fun and some might say "unproductive" behaviors, like sleep or a hike in the mountains, a massage, a good work-out, a phone chat with a girlfriend, or a picnic lunch on the waterfront. As one with a "good work ethic," I don't shy away from work or effort, but I used to identify my value with how much work I have accomplished and what results I have achieved. My actions were not aligned... they were compulsive! (I'm sure by now you know that the compulsions are veils.) I encourage you to be diligent about staying in Aligned Action. Be receptive and creative in the actions that propel you along your path.

Conviction and Grace

We must learn to trust that what needs to open within us will do so, in just the right fashion. In fact, our body, heart, and spirit know how to give birth, to open naturally, like the petals of a flower. We need not tear at the petals nor force the flower. We must simply stay planted and present.

— Jack Kornfield

With our big brains and our big, human egos, we are so easily tempted to thinking that we control everything — at least if we were doing it "right." But who's to say what right timing is? When I first began reading the works of Carl Jung, Thomas Moore, Marion Woodman and Joseph Campbell, I hadn't studied spirituality, the inner workings of the soul or the psyche, or Universal Principles. My understandings, up till then, were all intuitive and through what Jung may have said was from accessing the collective unconscious. There were things I knew that I didn't know why I knew them.

Then, as I read the works of these great healers, mystics and educators, I saw that much of what I read were things I knew.

"They know this, too?" I would think, "How amazing is that!"

Some of my innate *knowing* was of Universal Laws. Two I share with you here are the Law of Gestation, and the Law of Rhythm. Universal Laws speak to us through energy signatures, carrying the wisdom of all time and space. They can guide us to live in greater ease and grace. I choose these two to explore with you here as they may assist you in your integration of and personal understanding of the Sacred Truths.

The Law of Gestation

If you think about the gestation period that happens from the moment a sperm enters an egg and a fetus begins to form, and when that baby is born, you'll fully understand the Law of Gestation. There is an evolutionary process that must flow from one stage to the next in order to result in the birth of the baby. The same Law applies when you are evolving something new in yourself — or something that's totally new because it hasn't been invented yet. If you skip the development, if you're anxious and try to rush the process from insemination to new creation, what emerges is not usually sustainable.

Yes, you can move faster than is often thought. Scientists can show us how everything is energy, and time and space are illusions we conjured up so that we can perceive them. Paradoxically, the Law of Gestation says that we must allow ourselves to move through the process , eveloping into who and what we are becoming. Be patient with yourself and with Life when you are creating new experiences, new creations and a new perception of yourself. Remember that new life is often not pretty. There's loss and dissolution that must take place for the new life to emerge.

A caterpillar gives up everything it once was, becomes a pod of goo, and even as the metamorphosis is complete, the butterfly cannot fly until its wings are dry. "Surrender" in the spiritual sense is to "let go and let God." You will be called to surrender to the time and development that's required for your growth. (And continue to devotedly, diligently with Aligned Action.)

The Law of Rhythm

When you stand at the ocean's edge, you experience the rhythm of the waves. Coming in to the shore, water pours up onto the beach or splash upon rocks or cliffs, then perhaps seem to pause a moment before pouring back into the sea. If you stay a day or camp for several, you also see the tidal pulse, the rhythm of ocean, as it rises over time and then recedes.

Expand your gaze now to a broader view, and you notice the rhythm of the seasons.

Nature demonstrates the Law of Rhythm eloquently in all its subtleties and extremes. The earth-based cultures throughout time have known that there are more than the four primary seasons. There are the mid-points between them, and mid-points between those, each with characteristics and cycles of life. Each is required for the full cycle of life to unfold. We live those seasons, too, in our bodies, in our cultures, in our economies.

The Law of Rhythm tells us that all things change, continuously. What goes out must come in. As something contracts, it also expands, just as you do with your breath. There is perpetual motion, one expression or action leading to the next. All great literature and our world's religions through their scriptures and tomes, follow the Law of Rhythm. So, too, does soul-level transformation.

The Law of Rhythm says that we ebb and flow. While we aspire to grow at all times, growth is not just perpetual increase. Growth is contraction and expansion. If you are in a big growth or expansion phase, create room for your contraction, and know that contracting in this way is not the opposite of growth. It is the ebb to your flow. It may be that you need time to grieve or are called on to release aspects of your life that are challenging for you to let go of.

If you resist the ebb, it would be like a deciduous tree in autumn refusing to allow its leaves to wither and fall. It must allow this stage of life to take place — for what comes in winter will require it to have let go of what is "done." Winter is not a dead season. There is life happening all around. You simply may not be able to see it as it moves underground or more slowly in the quiet of the season.

Be patient with your Soul's Timing, as you ebb and flow in life.

To every thing there is a season,

and a time to every purpose under the heaven:

A time to be born, and a time to die;

a time to plant, and a time to pluck up that which is planted;

A time to kill, and a time to heal;

a time to break down, and a time to build up;

A time to weep, and a time to laugh;

a time to mourn, and a time to dance...

Ecclesiastes 3:1

There are beautiful balance points between desire and allowing, between giving joyously and opening to receive, between *being* and aligned action. Those mid-points are the intersections of Being Here Now. No forecasting or promoting change. Simply being.

An unveiled path continually reveals new joyous opportunities for living a life that has meaning and prosperity. As you travel this path, it will continue to appear before you. And, no matter how far along the path you go, you will find more veils. Many will even seem to reappear. When that happens, it is not because you are doing anything wrong. It doesn't mean that you are back to square one. It is simply that veils are often multi-layered. There is more of your radiant soul to be revealed to you and to the world. Working with a mentor who can guide you along your path is invaluable. Even with years of practice in your personal-spiritual journey, there is great benefit in receiving the gift of another's wisdom, witnessing and support. I have been witness and mentor to thousands of men and women as they have revealed their souls' radiance by removing layers that once defined them — while guiding them to embrace their Truths. I, too, have had many mentors, guides and peers along my journey. I celebrate the shared experiences those many relationships have made possible.

An unveiled path traverses a varied landscape. I invite you to step out along your path with conviction and in grace. I feel blessed to be on your journey with you, and to have you join me on mine.

I have a profound sense of awe and appreciation for this magnificent tapestry we call Life. Every moment of it is worthy of Celebration!

The section that follows offers a selection of Life-Integration Practices. You can use these practices — or be inspired by them to create your own. I offer you options for integrating Sacred Truths in both inner and outer expressions, soulful and applicable. As you know, simply reading practices does not facilitate change. You must also act, whether through reflection-contemplation, embodied imagination, an exercise or a task.

I welcome you to share with me your experiences with these or any Life-Integration Practices. (Find out how you can contact me in the Resources section at the end of the book.)

PART IV:
Life-Integration

Practices for Soul-Level Transformation

Several years ago I reached into a box that stores old journals. I'm not sure why I was looking in there, perhaps by some intuitive or inspired guidance. I pulled out a journal from 10-12 years ago. Holding it in two hands, I allowed it to fan open to a page mid way into the book. There I found a list I had written. A list I don't recall writing, but I do remember feeling the desires that were expressed. I read about the life I wanted to create, the life I wanted to be living. As I read, I realized that I could have written this same list, not as desires for something I didn't yet have in my life, but as a gratitude list for the things I love in my life. Everything I had written years before was my "now-reality." And I'm not just talking about outer-life manifestations like my home and my relationships. The qualities of how I experience LIFE on the inside, my perspectives, my self talk, the richness of my inner tapestry — that was what moved me to tears — and big, broad smiles.

I'm not really sure that I believed any of it was possible when I wrote that list. I do remember, though, the years of shoring up my courage to allow myself to even feel my desire, and then to express it. I read that page and was filled with such an appreciation for the journey my life has been — and for the "proof" I have that soul-level transformation is real. Life-Integration Practices are the tools I used along the way.

These Life-Integration Practices will support you as you integrate and live Sacred Truths. Notice if you are drawn to any of the practices.

What do you want to develop? Choose a practice that is designed to support that specifically. Commit to that practice for a period of time, depending on the practice and your intention. Commit to what it has to teach you, or to develop in you.

Please know, too, that these are not "quick-fix" tasks that you can use to create ego-gratifying change. It's easy to be tempted to think like that. Soul-level transformation is perhaps slower than you sometimes might want. Be patient with yourself and honest in your self-reflection as you grow and unveil to your radiance.

There are sacred teachings the world over that suggest a certain power and grace in the number 40. I suggest that as you begin a practice, be prepared to commit to it for 40 days. A new way of *being* requires an integrated perception of your environment. Practices are designed with the intention to alter your perception of your environment. That environment might be your thoughts, or your behaviors, your body, your physical surroundings, or your relationships — or the energy around you. Don't effort to change the "things." Instead create the change with your energy and your perception. That's where Life-Integration Practices come in.

Integrating the First Sacred Truth: You are Infinite and Powerful.

Meditation.

Learn and practice a form of meditation consistently.

Meditation is the most essential practice for integrating this Sacred Truth. Meditation challenges you to focus your attention, to commune with Source, to rise above your thoughts and ideas that tend to be overactive and clingy.

Practice will bring you into a new state of Being.

Contemplation.

Give yourself 5-10 minutes of contemplation.

Find a place outside where you can see the sky, or be near a tree or a body of water, or perhaps an art installation or a fountain — if you're in a city. Let yourself be drawn to recognize and appreciate the miracles around you. Experience the grace of this moment, your ability to feel, sense and perceive beauty. Allow yourself to be moved as you bring your attention and intention to a state of awe.

Discover Your Soul's Divine Purpose.

As with any practice, only **you** can truly choose to commit to your Purpose and the unfolding development that you will experience — what it requires of you.

While I work with some clients to discover and clarify their Souls' Divine Purpose, I highly recommend the work my dear friend, Tim Kelley, has done in this arena. His book, *True Purpose*, guides you through your own process to discover your Purpose and to continue to be informed, allowing your understanding and activation of purpose to grow as you do.

Other methods for exploring, confirming, grounding in or defining your Purpose include Hand Analysis, Astrology, Prayer, Active Imagination and Dreamwork. (Find links to people, books and programs I recommend and more I've created for you on http://TambraHarck.com

Life-Integration Practice Ideas.

- Look for Spiritual Sustenance: Seek and partake in what feeds your Spiritual Self. (Perhaps you are fed through other people, nature, films, music, conversation, reading, devotional practice, travel, going on retreat.)
- Commit to living in accord with your Purpose.

- Develop skills and resources to support you in giving more expression to your Purpose.
- Work with a spiritual teacher to ground your own understanding and expression of yourSelf as the Infinite and Powerful Being that you are.
- Exercise your power of choice: It's your decision.
- Create and experience rituals that deepen and heighten your remembrance of who you truly are.
- Journal: Dialog with your Higher Self or the Divine.
- Watch films that express this message in various ways such as: *The Living Matrix, What the Bleep Do We Know?*, or *Powers of 10*.
- Practice dreamwork and other methods of soulful exploration. (I share more about dream work in videos you can see on my website at http://TambraHarck.com/watch)

Integrating the Second Sacred Truth: Your Body is the Temple of Your Soul.

Body-Wisdom Dialogue.

Begin a dialog or active imagination with your body with an openness of mind and heart.

- When you begin this practice, I recommend that you set a sacred space and time for it. There is no rush. (It's not speed dating...) It's not that your body is slow so much as you are not accustomed to listening to it in this way.
- First, set an intention.
- Then you might dance freely for a while to create a connection and awareness in your movements.
- With a journal, drawing paper and colors, sculpting clay, or even a stick in the dirt, begin an active imagination with your body. Remain curious, open and allowing as you ask open questions, and listen for the way you receive replies.
- You will probably find that while your body can answer yes-no questions, these are not questions that will engage you in a conversation. Imagine that you are talking with someone, wanting to get to know her, sharing yourself and your interests, inquiring about hers.
- When you make agreements with your body, keep them. If you cannot keep them, or fail to, be honest about it.

Your body is wise beyond your imagination. Ask how your body can support you in making agreements that you will keep.

•

Life-Integration Practice Ideas.

- Choose one practice from the Body-Wisdom I shared in the chapter on this Sacred Truth on pages 44-47. Create your own personal rituals or habits to embody the practice, that you may be informed and enriched by it.
- Look to your physical environments. Are they supporting you in living, being, expressing your authentic voice? If so, appreciate and tend to them. If not, choose a space that you will transform, bringing it into alignment with the radiance of your soul.
- Dance. Attend dance and movement classes that invite you to move your body in a way that guides you to soul-level connection. A few examples I recommend are: *TransDance* classes in Berkeley, CA, taught by my friend and temple dancer, Heather Munro Pierce; *5Rhythms* or *Sweat Your Prayers* classes, originated by Gabrielle Roth, and now led by certified teachers around the world; some teachers who offer *NIA*-inspired classes; *Authentic Movement* programs.

- Engage in an ongoing, committed practice that honors and integrates mind-body-soul-spirit such as yoga, chi gong, aikido, tai chi or acupuncture.
- Create or participate in rituals by yourself or in sacred community. Examples might include trance-dancing, sweat lodges or prayer circles that bring voice and movement into your prayers.
- See an energy healer regularly.
- Follow a detox program. You can detoxify your body, your environment, your daily schedule, your relationships, even your business. (NOTE: Having a plan and the support of someone who can skillfully and objectively support or guide you is highly beneficial when you engage in a detoxification program. Of any sort.)
- Take a sound-healing class.
- Develop sensitive awareness of your subtle-body energy. (Links to recommended videos on YouTube created by my colleague, Gurutej, can be found in the Resource section at the back of book.)
- Join me in a private retreat or at a BodyWisdom Retreat.

Integrating the Third Sacred Truth: Soul Desire is Your Unique Key to the Universe.

Attune to the Resonance of Your Soul Desire.

Practice attuning to your experience of Soul Desire. Become sensitively aware of the ways that you personally and energetically experience your Desire.

Embodied Imagination.

When you have a clear picture or idea of a Soul Desire, bring the experience alive in your body; activate it with your imagination.

- Begin by standing, your feet hips distance apart or a little wider, knees slightly bent.
- Close your eyes.
- Bring your attention to your Soul Desire. As best you can, open to the resonance or energy vibration that brings it more fully into your awareness.
- Notice if there is a response in your body, perhaps a tingle, warmth, shivers, a flutter or contraction that resonates in you as you focus on your Soul Desire. You may sense this as a color or shift in temperature or an image.

- Bring your softened attention to this area in or on or around your body.
- As you draw your awareness of your body and your Soul Desire into vividness, begin to imagine that your desire is now your reality.
- Allow your body to be moved as you move in this new reality. Physically experience and imagine yourself in the time and space of your desire manifested.
- Be curious and patient. Ask that your Soul move you and guide your imagination, bringing you through experiences, seeing, sensing, feeling yourself change, adapt and grow in the ways that will bring you into this new reality.
- Imagine you are there, fully realized in your Desire. It's real. It's now. Step into it. What is it like to live in this new experience? How do you move, what do you see, who are you with? Actually move your body, feel sensations, make gestures that you imagine will be your experience as this Desire is Reality.
- As you complete, let your movements slowly come to stillness.
- You may wish to journal or draw or voice record or somehow "concretize" or embody the experience.

When practicing Embodied Imagination, you may also want to play some music. Choose either a piece that is neutral like meditation music, or if you are aware of a sound or a specific piece of music that attunes you to your Soul Desire, choose that. (And play the latter often!)

Life-Integration Practice Ideas.

- Begin a Soul Desire journal. Record your experiences of the resonance of your desire. Write only of what you want. Imagine you are living it right now and write about it. How do you feel? What is it like to be a living expression of your desire? (If you find that thoughts of doubt and judgment hijack your writing, you can create a special section in your journal for those thoughts, and work with them later. Using the Discernment Process can help uncover and remove veils.)
- Listen and feel, sense and awaken to your Desire. Be curious and courageous with what's revealed to you. You may be surprised by and unfamiliar with what you discover.
- Ask a trusted person in your life or a mentor to witness your declaration of a Soul Desire.
- Work with a mentor to help you feel, sense, recognize and follow your Soul Desire; and to live into it.

- Ask upon waking, or in meditation, "What do I want?" If you could truly feel your desire, what would it be? Then listen and feel for an answer. Trust your Self to know. (One man who participated in a training program with me about 10 years ago started with an even simpler version of this practice. Each day when he considered what he wanted for his next meal, he stopped a moment, made a conscious connection with him-Self and asked, "What do I want to eat?" When he heard the answer, his next step in this practice was to then tell his wife, "I want _____." He wanted to develop the ability to ask, listen to his answer, and then express what he wanted. After a short time he felt more confidence in his ability, and ask, "What do I want?" in a more expanded way.)

Integrating the Fourth Sacred Truth: Love Is.

Body-Energizer of Love.

Use this practice to develop a connection to Divine Love and to experiencing Self Love.

This practice can be done as you finish meditation, as you wake, just before sleep, or at any time you wish to ground the physical experience of the energy of Love in your body. For example, if you are using this practice to complete your sitting meditation:

- Extend your arms in front of your body so that your hands are at chest level. Hands cupped together, as you would if you were letting them fill with water to splash on your face, raise them above your head, imagining that as you lift your hands they are scooping up the energy of Love.
- Feel, see and sense this as real.
- Allow Love to pour from your hands onto your head, shoulders and body.
- Say aloud, "This is Love, Source-essence of all Creation. I am showered with Love, receiving its energy and many blessings."
- Continue, repeating the gesture of cupping your hands, bringing them to your forehead, then your eyes, your lips-jaw-throat, your heart and chest, the length of your

body — between your solar plexus and your pelvis, continuing to your legs and feet, arms and hands. With each area of your body, modify the blessing.

An example for your lips-jaw-throat might be to say, "These are the lips of Love, Source-essence of all Creation. My lips, mouth, jaw and voice are messengers and recipients of Love. Love infuses me and the world around me as I speak, eat, kiss, hear, and creatively express myself."

Breath of Love.

Use this practice to develop an experience of any or all of the Four Powers of Love.

This is a breathing practice you can do at any time, as meditation, alone, with another person, or with a group. (I invite you to set the book down now for a few moments and give yourself this experience. Even if you think you know what it will be, try it.)

- Sit or stand comfortably. Feel your feet flat on the floor. Allow yourself to be supported and held by the earth beneath you. If you are lying down, feel the places on your body where you are in contact with the surface that is holding you.

- Close your eyes.
- Simply draw your attention to your breath. Allow your focus to move with the sensation as you receive your breath. Feel your body sensations and movements as your breath expands, and as you release it.
- Bring your attention to the experience of inhaling. See, sense, feel the air as it comes in through your nose or mouth, filling your lungs. Imagine now that each breath carries a stream of love that flows into your body. Receive your breath, as you receive and circulate love. Experience your breath as Love. Allow your imagination to support you in this as you inhale, breathing in Love. You may see an image with Breath of Love, or a color. Maybe you hear a sound or remember the sensation of a time when you felt nourished by love. Or perhaps you imagine that your breath inflates a flower in your heart, or your cells may be drinking at the river of Love. It's your experience. Simply breathe Love.
- As you exhale, allow your breath to move freely from your nose or mouth, sending Love out into the air around you. Love flows out, offering it freely that it may serve wherever it is needed. Again, use embodied imagination to make the experience of exhaling Love real for you. Perhaps you'll see your breath sending ribbons of Love, swirling out into the air and space that

surrounds you, your home, your family, your business or all around the planet, even out into the galaxy or beyond. You may even choose to direct Love as prayer, sending it to a person, place or thing.

- Inhale Love, allowing the energy of Love to heal, soothe, inspire, calm and center you. Exhale Love, freely sending it back to original source. Breathe in Love. Breathe out Love.
- When you have breathed love for a few minutes you may feel lightheaded or giddy. Or you may feel a sense of grief or loss. Tears may well up in your eyes. You may even begin to sob. Just let any feelings be there, and let Love flow with your breath.

Life-Integration Practice Ideas.

- Contemplate a loving Universe, God, Life-Force, the source and meaning of Divine Love.
- Practice Heart-Centered meditation or other meditations grounded in Love. (You will find the Breath of Love, a complimentary guided meditation and training, on my website at http://TambraHarck.com/lovegift.)
- Choose Love. Begin and end each day with "I Choose Love." Say it repeatedly throughout your day, say aloud

to yourself, This mantra will raise your awareness over time, and maybe even change your brain! Choose Love.

- Begin a Love Journal. Write in it daily about what you love. What it feels like to experience love. Imagine and remember, feel and think of love in all forms — Divine Love, self-love, and your love of another or of a place or an object. Open to and recall the experience of receiving love — from another or a place in nature, a temple or a meal. Play and draw your experiences of love with appreciation and wonder.
- Ask, "I wonder... if I loved myself in this moment, what would be different? How would I be, how would I feel, what choice would I make...?" Listen for the reply. Then, move into that experience.
- Create a conscious, disciplined practice for supreme, loving self-care.
- Practice deep appreciation before each meal. Appreciate the food before you, and your body's ability to receive nourishment. Appreciate the sounds, scents, textures, colors of your meal. Appreciate that you are dining alone, or that you are sharing a meal with others.
- Write love letters to yourself on exquisite stationery. Mail them. Read them. Keep them in a beautiful box.

- Fall in love with your life. Love your work. Love your body. Love your Purpose. Love your ambition. Love your past. Love your possibility. Love now.
- Join a Speaking Circle. (See Resources in back of book to discover a meeting near you.)
- Practice being present and open-hearted while you are with another person.
- Look at those around you through eyes of Love.
- Attend classes or retreats for developing intimacy, sensuality, sexuality or communication with a beloved.
- Review the list of Expressions of Loving and Being Loved on pages 89-90, and choose one that creates a stirring in you as a practice.
- Collaborate on a creative project with someone.
- Be of service to the WellBeing of others; perhaps by tutoring a neighbor, volunteering for a clean-up project, planting trees in a park, starting a service foundation or singing at a hospice center. Allow your intuition to show you how and where to serve.
- Write a letter to send with your donations to charitable organizations, filling the letter with the energy of Love. You can do this even if your donations are given anonymously.

- Work with a mentor to create a practice that will help you integrate the *Sacred Truth: Love Is* fully in your being.
- Listen to *Joy of Love and Life* podcast. (Listen to my shows with a yearning to experience Love. Find the show on iTunes, just search "Joy of Love and Life.")
- Practice embodied energy techniques to remove unconscious and environmental blocks to Love.

Integrating the Fifth Sacred Truth: You Are Not Your Veils.

"I Am" Meditation.

Combining breath awareness and a form of a mantra, this meditation brings you to yourSelf, releasing that which is *not* you simply by focusing your attention with two words: I Am.

- To begin, sit or stand with your feet on the floor. Draw your breath into your lower abdomen first, then allow your lower lungs to fill, and finally your chest.
- Exhaling in the same order, gently squeeze your breath out from your lower abdomen, your mid-section, and then from your chest. Keep your shoulders down and back, the front of your chest open.
- After a few breaths like this, as you become familiar and comfortable with the breath, imagine on your inhale that the air is not contained in your body. Inhale into your abdomen, torso and chest, and sense, see and feel that it expands beyond you into the space around you. Exhale returning to your "size" or the boundaries of your body.
- Repeat this breath and imagery another few cycles.
- Now, on the next inhale, say to yourself, hear the sound of your own voice, saying, "I."
- Exhale with the sound of the word, silently, "Am."

- I — Inhale.
- Am — Exhale.
- I — Inhale.
- Am — Exhale.
- Continue for five minutes or longer.

You may also use this practice during yoga or while walking, or when starting to feel reactive. Just modify your breathing to suit the activity. (When I first intuitively began this meditation, I was in an Authentic Movement class. I explored the textures and contours of the room with my touch, saying, "I Am." I took it on as a personal practice soon after. I have since taught this to clients who have used it before having what they anticipated would be a difficult conversation. Others have shared with me that I Am has led them to emotional releases of long-held grief, shame and anger.) I encourage you to practice it and see what develops for you.

Life-Integration Practice Ideas.

- Declutter and Release. Remove from your environment excesses that do not promote your growth and WellBeing. Eliminate any reflections of *what you're not* from your environment.

- Create personal rituals that give you a sense of Self. You may choose to begin or end each day by reading spiritual passages, or in contemplation of the blessings and graces that appeared in your life. Or you may say aloud to another five things for which you are grateful, feeling your gratitude — beyond the words.
- Contemplate the question, "How have I closed my heart today?" Simply listen to the answers, and the underlying motivations that led you to close your heart. Practice forgiving yourself. Look to the veils of those motivations. Are you willing to release them?
- Learn and practice using energy tools for clearing.
- Surround yourself with people who are life-affirming in their actions, words and presence.
- Expose yourself to brilliance — read, listen to, converse, study, partner with...
- Create rituals that increase your visions of the future.
- Incorporate practices and rituals into your daily life that enhance your feelings about the now.
- Tell the truth. Lifting the veils that perpetuate lies you have been telling yourself and others about whom and how you are is profoundly enriching. Begin with telling your truth. Honesty with yourself first, and then with the people in your life, sets you free.

- Practice intentional appreciation. Each day look for what you appreciate and then share it with another, saying it aloud, bringing yourself into the feeling state (the energy) of your appreciation.
- Express Gratitude, expanding into experiences of profound Appreciation. Your practice may to state and feel your gratitude each day upon rising or before sleep.
- Celebrate your awesomeness.

Integrating the Sixth Sacred Truth: Believe. Act in Faith. Trust.

Create and Engage with an Altar.

An altar can be a physical external reflection of that which you Believe. Remember, to Believe is to "be in accord with Love, Life." You may choose to create an altar to honor your love of family, or your value for growing and learning, or your desire for something that you hold dear. It can be created or found anywhere. Choose a location for your altar that fits with its intention and how you will engage with it.

- Clarify the purpose or intention of your altar. Is it intended for prayer or meditation? Will you use it for devotional reading? Is it an altar to honor your family and ancestry? Do you want it to remind you of your values, your dreams or your connection to the Divine? Is it an altar that will support you in developing something new, such as a relationship, inner peace, or clarity of mind? Clarify your intention first.
- Choose a location for your altar. The purpose or intention may readily tell you where It will be located. How much space do you need for it? Is it private, or will you share this altar with others — whether they use it or not? (I have a meditation altar in the living room of our

home. Anyone is welcome to sit there for his or her practice.) It can be in your home, office, bedroom, garden, on a hearth, a meditation table, a windowsill or your desk.

- Let yourself be guided to select the items that will be on this altar.
  - Will you choose to have the elements (fire, earth, air, water, ether) represented by altar objects? Is it a location outside, under a tree, at the edge of a brook, in a local park?
  - You may find that a collection of photographs — of your family, friends, community, clients, projects, landscape, animals, or architecture — will be the objects that best align with the energetic intention for this altar.
  - This altar might be supporting you in developing a new capacity, skill or perspective. If so, you might include objects that represent development and mastery in that area. For instance, opening to the Divine Feminine, you may choose a statue of Kwan Yin, Mother Mary, or Gaia, an open challis or pitcher, an image of a volcano, a loving letter written to you by your grandmother.
- Sometimes sacred space or an altar serves its purpose simply by its existence. More often, though, it is essential

that you engage with it. You may want to set a structure or create a ritual that supports your participation with the energy and intention of your altar.

Life-Integration Practice Ideas.

- Commit to a Soul Desire that you want to experience as Reality. Act in Faith.
- Pray with praise.
- Be bold, diligent and decisive as you live each day. Unwaveringly pursue your highest calling.
- Listen to your inner guidance or intuition, and act on it: Act in Faith.
- Practice Forgiveness. Focus daily in a prayerful way on the question, "How have I closed my heart today?" Did you close your heart to yourself, to your connection to the Divine, or to another person in reaction, judgment, hurt or anger? Imagine this person — even if it is you, standing before you, bathed in radiant light. Release the veils that kept you from seeing this person as the miracle he or she is. Allow compassion to rise in you. Allow your heart to open once again. Feel gratitude for the miracle of forgiveness.
- If you are challenged with trusting yourself, create a practice of forgiveness to help you shift the energy and

your experience of what it means, and how it feels to live in a state of self-trust-worthiness.

- Get an accountability buddy. Each day plan a 10-minute conversation with one another. Take turns as you go through each of these steps: 1) What I'm celebrating about myself is... 2) What I said I would be/do yesterday that I was/did...; and what I said I would be/do and wasn't/didn't... 3) Today I will... The goal here is to be a witness and have a witness, not to process each other. Periodically you may ask for feedback or support or brainstorming as well.

Integrating the Call to Continue

Listen to Your Intuition.

Intentionally tune into your intuition, building confidence and competence as you become more aware of and respond to intuitive information.

Over the course of 21 consecutive days, at least three times each day, intentionally listen to your intuition, and let it guide you. Intuitively stand in front of the elevator door you think will open. Call that person who comes to mind. Draw a tarot card and without looking at the face of the card, intuit what card it is, or what the energy/meaning of the card is. Keep an ongoing journal to record how you experience your intuition, what it's telling you, and how you're responding to it, as well as what unfolds.

Commit to Tithing

The practice of Tithing is a Universal Law. Make a commitment to tithe 10%, or if that is not the number you will personally "stand behind," choose the percentage that you will. For you it may be 5% or 20%. The important part of this practice is to commit to it, and then to take the actions on your commitment.

Once you choose the percentage of your income and windfalls that you will tithe, decide how and to whom you will make your offerings. You may want to tithe to your church or temple, or your spiritual teacher. You may, as Edwene Gaines discusses in her book, *The Four Spiritual Laws of Prosperity,* choose to tithe to that which feeds you spiritually, and to prayerfully consider to whom you will give or send your tithing. I have heard Andrew Harvey, the spiritual activist, a man with a fine mind and burning heart, say that he tithes by giving to a cause that has deep meaning for him.

You choose. Then participate, intentionally, soulfully, with your ongoing commitment to tithe. No matter how little or how much money comes into you life, tithing will enrich you and the world in ways you may not even be able to imagine!

An Exercise in Joyous Prosperity.

Where in your life do you want to experience Joyous Prosperity? How do you feel wealthy, abundant, rich? Take a soulful approach to your inquiry. Your soul speaks through image, sensation, play, imagination, symbol, nature, fantasy, dance, poetry, art, music, dreams, intuition.

Feel, sense, see or imagine yourself as joyously prosperous. Then ask: How may I experience even more Joyous Prosperity? Areas of your life you may wish to look at include:

- Spiritually
- Physically
- Sensually
- Sexually
- Creatively
- Financially
- Relationally
- Intimately
- Mentally
- Community
- Professionally
- Environmentally
- add to this list ________
- ________________

Record your answers or replies through journaling, using art supplies or your voice. Allow yourself to be informed, surprised, inspired!

Practice the Power of Discernment.

Use the Discernment Process when you are making decisions and pondering opportunities. You may want to use a journal to walk yourself through the steps of the process. (You'll find the full process described on pages 165-167

- Write until you are clear about the question you are asking.
- Then at the top of a page, state your question or opportunity.
- Write each question in Step 2.
- Record your answers.
- The next step is to choose.
- The decision you make puts you and the Universe in motion. If you waffle on your decision, the Universe will vibrationally reflect your indecision. Be courageous, curious, compassionate and clear.

Soul-Level Discovery Using the Power of Discernment.

If you want to use the Discernment Process for soulful questions, modify your approach. Allow the process to guide you through a series of inquiries that may bring you wisdom, insight, or energetic shifts. Ask your questions through dance, art, music, dreams, active imagination and other interpretations of the Language of Your Soul.

A Blessing

The spark of vitality that lives in you
is a miracle that only you can bring to life.

Your life is a miracle moment to moment to moment.

Open your channels of Divinity, Vitality and Soul Desire,
Be guided along your own path with an abundance of joy, meaning and love.

My hand at my heart, I look into your eyes, as I bow and say to you,

This, my friend, is your Life.
I see and celebrate the essence of you.
Namaste!

I wish I could speak like music.
I wish I could put the swaying splendor
Of the fields into words
So that you could hold Truth
Against your body
And dance.

I am trying the best I can
With this crude brush, the tongue,
To cover you with light.
I wish I could speak like divine music.
I want to give you the sublime rhythms
Of this earth and the sky's limbs
As they joyously spin and surrender,

Surrender
Against God's luminous breath.
God wants you to hold me
Against your precious
Body
And dance,
Dance.

— Hafiz

References

An Unveiled Path

Arch Bishop Desmond Tutu: quoted in *The NPR Interviews* edited by Robert Siegel, 1994.
Joseph Campbell: *The Power of Myth,* (Anchor, 1991).

An Intuitive Discovery

David Whyte: *House of Belonging,* (Harper Collins, 1981).

A New Humanity

Paul H. Ray and Sherry Ruth Anderson: *Cultural Creatives,* (Harmony Books, 2000).

The First Sacred Truth

Chandogya Upanishad: *The Upanishads,* translated by Juan Mascaro, (Penguin Classics, 1965).
Agnes de Mille: *Martha: The Life and Work of Martha Graham,* (Random House, 1991).
Richard Unger: *LifePrints, (Crossing Press, 2007).*
Mark Robert Waldman: in a live presentation at *TEDxConejo Conference,* March 2010.

The Second Sacred Truth

St. Teresa von Avila: *The Life of St. Teresa of Avila,* (Cosimo, 2006)
Joseph Campbell, *The Power of Myth,* (Anchor, 1991).
Marion Woodman, in an interview for O *Magazine,* September 2009.

The Third Sacred Truth

Ralph Waldo Emerson: *The Works of Ralph Waldo Emerson, Vol VI, Poems,* (John D. Morris & Co., 1906).
Paulo Coelho, *The Alchemist,* (Editora Rocco Limited, 1988).

The Fourth Sacred Truth

Sophocles: Oedipus at Colonus

The Fifth Sacred Truth

Swami Vivekanada: The Upanishads: Volume IV, (no publisher, 1994).
Jelaluddin Rumi: *The Essential Rumi,* translated by Coleman Barks, (HarperOne, 1997).

The Sixth Sacred Truth

Myrtle Fillmore: *Letters of Myrtle Fillmore,* (Unity Classic Library, 2008).
Johann Wolfgang Von Goethe: *Faust,* (New American Library, 1958)
Gregg Levoy: *Callings, Finding and Following an Authentic Life* (Three Rivers Press, 1998).
Martin Luther King, Jr.: (unattributed or unconfirmed).
Jack Armstrong: Lessons from the Source, (iUniverse, 2008).

The Call to Continue

William Faulkner: *Address upon Receiving the Nobel Prize for Literature,* Stockholm, December 1950, as quoted in *Storied Inquiries in International Landscapes,* edited by Tonya Huber, (Information Age Publishing, 2010).

Joyous Prosperity

Woodrow Wilson: *Address at Swarthore College,* December 1913, as quoted in *Selected Addresses and Public Papers of Woodrow Wilson*, edited by Albert Bushnell Hart, (Modern Publisher, 1918).
Richard Bach: *The Bridge Across Forever,* (Dell, 1989).
Wallace Wattles: *The Science of Getting Rich,* (originally published in 1910).

How Much Can You Bare?

Kahlil Gibran: *The Prophet,* (Alfred A. Knopf, 1970).

The Power of Discernment

Carl Jung: *Memories, Dreams, Reflections, (Pantheon Books of NY, 1989).*

Breaking Free

Jelaluddin Rumi: *The Essential Rumi,* translated by Coleman Barks, (HarperOne, 1997).
Ibid.

Co-Creating Your Life

Albert Einstein: (unattributed or unconfirmed).

With Conviction and Grace

Jack Kornfield: *The Path with Heart*, (Bantam, 1993).
Ecclesiastes: *The Holy Bible*, (King James Version).

Practices for Soul-Level Transformation

Edwene Gaines: *The Four Spiritual Laws of Prosperity*, (Holtzbrink Publishers, 2005).
Andrew Harvey: *The Hope*, (Hay House, Inc., 2007).
Hafiz: *The Gift*, translated Daniel Ladinsky, (The Penguin Group, 1999).

Resources

Recommended Reading
Callings by Gregg Levoy
Care of the Soul by Thomas Moore
God Works Through Faith by Dr. Robert A. Russell
The Four Spiritual Laws of Prosperity by Edwene Gaines
The Hope by Andrew Harvey
Lessons from the Source by Jack Armstrong
The Practice of Awakening II by Paul Hoyt
Loving What Is by Byron Katie
The Science of Getting Rich by Wallace Wattles
The Infinite Wisdom of the Akashic Records by Lisa Barnett
True Purpose by Tim Kelley
A Whole New Mind by Daniel Pink
The 7 Graces of Marketing by Lynn Serafinn
Love for No Reason by Marci Schimoff
The Soul of Money by Lynne Twist
Emotional Balance by Dr Roy Martina

Videos and Films
The Energy Gurus Series on YouTube. Gurutej leads you through easy, effective energy-body exercises
The Shift, starring Wayne Dyer
The Living Matrix, featuring Lynne McTaggert
I Am – The Documentary by Tom Shadyac

You will find links to a variety of videos I've made for you – at http://TambraHarck.com/watch.

Additional Colleagues and Organizations Recommended
Speaking Circles International
Find out more at www.speakingcircles.com

Village Empowerment
Spread Love Around the World by supporting Don Smith's efforts at http://VillageEmpowerment.com

TransDance with Heather Munro Pierce in Berkeley, CA
Find out more at www.templeartsinstitute.com

Join Tambra

Nu Wisdom School

For some of us, our studies and integration of deep wisdom is what brings us more fully *To Life*. This is my life's path and why I founded Nu Wisdom School where we explore our unique and collective expressions of bridging Heaven and Earth. Find out about upcoming curriculum and how you can join me and others from around the world by visiting http://nuWisdomSchool.com

Private Retreats

If you would like to work with me personally, to integrate what you've read in *Sacred Truths,* or in your spirit, body, desire, heart, mind, soul, environment, business or creative expressions, simply request information by sending an email to: office@TambraHarck.com

Keynote & Guest Speaking

With her warm, intuitive and engaging presence, Tambra is a highly appreciated speaker, inspiring audiences and congregations to soulful alignment and courageous action. If you would you like to see Tambra speak at your upcoming conference, convention or spiritual gathering, send an email to office@TambraHarck.com with your inquiry.

Online Courses, Meditations & Activations

Integrating these Sacred Truths is easier and more fun when we share the experiences in sacred community. So each year Tambra offers a unique program online where you can connect with others who are living and learning and contributing, too. You'll find previous popular courses, meditations and energy activations at http://TambraHarck.com.

Listen to Podcasts, Watch Videos
You'll find ***Joy of Love and Life*** on iTunes where Tambra engages with other spiritual leaders in intimate conversations. Guests share insights from New Thought to Ancient Wisdom, from Prosperity to Philanthropy, from Relationships to Paths of Devotion.

nuVolutions podcast welcomes you to discover yourself among the millions of unique souls who are issuing humanity into new possibility. Hear about and meet others who are in the 5 Soul Groups of this "time of great change."

You Are U Symposium brings you into revealing conversations to deepen your self awareness and the important, timely role you play in the world today. Exploring topics such as "Know Thyself," and "Your Vitality and WellBeing," Tambra and her guests create practical and inspired connections and welcome you into the experience.

Contact Tambra at:
office@TambraHarck.com

Acknowledgements

I am profoundly grateful for the love and wisdom of the many souls who have made enormous contributions to me, my life and this work, including:

Every writer who has had the courage, tenacity and audacity to write and publish a book; you paved a reality before me. I have more appreciation for you than you can know.

My many teachers and mentors, some of whom I never met, yet have been deeply touched by since an early age.

Each client and student who were, in turn, my teachers — you shared your journeys with me, and have been a part of mine.

The many who have been alongside me at times through this journey – whose eyes lit up when I said I was writing (or re-releasing) this book; and my beloved Soul-Sisters, Diane Fleck, Teresa Owen, Atim Kavi, Margo Sims, Pam Taylor, Renee Baribeau, and Irene Hughes.

Countless friends and clients who've declared, "Tambra, please, you need to write a book!" David Neagle for reflecting to me something of my highest calling — in such a way that could no longer resist Truth. And Baeth Davis for saying it like it is. Immense gratitude for each of you.

I am grateful to the human-angels whose attention, encouragement and skill were essential to me in writing Sacred Truths. Sandy Pendleton, your generosity and forthrightness helped me wrap my mind around the potential of a book and its form. Karen Frank, you showed up to play with me in the creative sandbox that first day when the inspiration of this book began; without either of us knowing it. Jan Tallent, your editing skills on the first edition of Sacred Truths aided me in seeing it all the way through. Kathryn Bing-You, your insights helped reshape the flow and structure of this book in ways that help me believe in it anew.

Marissa Berger, who turned my doodles into dimension and flow. Jim Balkovek: I have forever appreciated your talent as an illustrator, and am honored to have it grace the cover of this book. Marilynn Collin, your love of photography and delight in capturing my image has been a gift beyond our decades of friendship.

Auntie Em (Emma Lou James), you saw the truth of who I am and I saw you seeing me. In that moment, veils that had kept me from my grace fell away – and perhaps healed ancestral wounds that spanned time long before we were here.

Rosalie Harck: No words express the depth or meaning of my appreciation. Thank you for being my mother, my friend, my student, champion and fellow traveler.

Michael, my love: You saw my soul, my path, and my contribution to Life the first day we met. Thank you for being my partner, my co-creator of beauty and adventure.

About the Author

Think *Practical Idealism* and you have a sense of Tambra Harck and her unique way in this world.

As a Deep-Wisdom Teacher and Speaker, Tambra blends mystical and material worlds. She presents innovative ways to bring people and possibilities together in service to humanity and all of Life.

She has been known as a *Divine Connector.* Her ability to see through divinity and make connections for people brings us all closer to The Divine. She connects people with each other and to the ideas, resources and wisdom that best serves their path.

For more than 30 years, Tambra has inspired clients, students and audiences to access their highest expressions, and to live soulful, joyous and contributing lives. A life-long vision has guided her to found ***NuWisdom***, a mystery school for our time. At *NuWisdom,* souls from around the planet gather to usher in new ways of living, leading and loving. They come together to answer a collective calling to experience 'heaven on earth' now and in the unfolding of time. Find out more about *NuWisdom* school, retreats and private programs at http://TambraHarck.com

A California native, Tambra now lives on Whidbey Island in Washington state with her sweetheart-partner, Michael. As a family, they build, plant and create beauty, basking in constant reminders of the rhythms and wonders of nature.

Notes

www.ingramcontent.com/pod-product-compliance
Lightning Source LLC
LaVergne TN
LVHW091047080826
845145LV00002B/649

* 9 7 8 0 6 1 5 3 8 9 5 8 5 *